Getting a Job in Europe

Getting a Job in Europe

The guide to finding short or long-term employment in Europe

MARK HEMPSHELL

4th edition

How To Books

By the same author

Finding Voluntary Work Abroad
Getting a Job in Travel and Tourism
Working as an Au Pair
Working in Hotels and Catering
Your own Business in Europe

Published by How To Books Ltd,
3 Newtec Place, Magdalen Road,
Oxford OX4 1RE, United Kingdom.
Tel: (01865) 793806. Fax: (01865) 248780.
email: info@howtobooks.co.uk
http://www.howtobooks.co.uk

Fourth edition revised and updated 2000

British Library Cataloguing in Publication Data.
A catalogue record for this book is available from the British Library.

Cover design by Shireen Nathoo Design
Cover image by PhotoDisc
Cover copy by Sallyann Sheridan
Cartoons by Mike Flanagan

Produced for How To Books by Deer Park Productions
Typeset by Anneset, Weston-super-Mare, N Somerset
Printed and bound by Cromwell Press, Trowbridge, Wiltshire

Contents

List of Illustrations

Preface
to the Fourth Edition

When the first edition of this book appeared several years ago, the concept of a single European jobs market was still something of a distant dream. But now, the necessary changes in both law and attitude have been made so that dream is now reality! There are more opportunities to work in Europe than there ever have been before!

It is easy to think that this is really nothing special. Whatever you do, don't be complacent! Europe is a massive and relatively united community of 360 million people offering millions of jobs. And you have the right, if you so wish, to take every advantage of that!

The fact is, it is now *almost* as easy to work in Berlin as Birmingham – or Rome as Renfrew. And many people – students, young people, executives and casual workers – are taking advantage of all the opportunities and doing just that.

If anything, the far greater number of opportunities to work in Europe have made finding your job rather harder. You need a guide to help you – and this book sets out to offer the help you need to find your job and settle down, temporarily or permanently, in another European country.

Of course, Europe as a united community is not an issue that will stand still. Further developments, such as the single European currency – or Euro – are being introduced in most (if not all) of the countries of the EU over the next few years. These are bound to have an effect on the jobs market, but as yet it is not entirely sure how.

However, no matter what you might feel about a united Europe as a political concept – this book makes no judgement on that issue – this has all been excellent news for the employment market today. The fact remains that Europeans now have access to incredible work and career opportunities that no other community anywhere else in the world – not even the US – can match.

All you need is the information, the talent and the determination to take up the opportunities on offer. The aim of this book is to provide you with the information.

Finally, as ever, I should say something about that which the politicians and bureaucrats can't change: that is the individual culture of the different countries in Europe. Every country is still very different culturally, and will probably always remain that way.

The most notable cultural difference you will encounter is the language, which can vary nationally and even regionally too. Whilst English is a leading world language and you can get work abroad speaking no other language, you will increase the opportunities open to you *multi-fold* if you can speak the local language of the country you wish to work in.

Finally, my grateful thanks go to the many people who have provided up-to-date information for this newest edition of *Getting a Job in Europe.* I do hope you will find it useful in taking advantage of all that Europe offers.

Mark Hempshell

1

Destination Europe

WHAT POSSIBILITIES ARE THERE?

Many people dream of working abroad. More often than not it is a dream of working in a sunny country. The land of opportunity — the USA — is also a popular potential destination. Comparatively few people think of working in continental Europe as their first choice. 'Too wet', 'too boring', 'too much like home' are typical comments.

However, Europe must actually now rank as the easiest region of the world to find a good job; in many cases much easier than getting a job in the UK itself. In a continent of two million square miles there has to be the right job for almost everyone, somewhere in Europe.

No matter what sort of work you want to do you should be able to find it in Europe, and find it more readily than in either the USA (which is quite difficult to emigrate to now) or in any sunny country of the world. Europe offers both casual jobs, and the top career jobs. It offers jobs in cities which are ready for the year 2000, and jobs in quiet rural areas or near sunsoaked beaches.

There really isn't any need to go anywhere outside Europe. It is just a matter of finding the right place for you.

COULD I DO IT?

It is fair to say that, nowadays, finding a job in Europe has become a practical proposition. However, so much depends on the individual. Most people will be able to find a job in Europe, but whether it is of the type they prefer or in the exact location they would like is a different matter.

Few people will be able to pick one particular job in one specific city or town and go out and get it. You need to be flexible. The country and the type of job you end up in may not be the one you had in mind when you started. In fact, it might well not be.

When considering possibilities there are two options to consider:

Work in the EU

The general principle is that nationals of one EU country are entitled to live and work in any other EU country. You cannot be prevented by national laws or different local qualifications or standards from working in

- France
- Germany
- Belgium
- Netherlands
- Luxembourg
- Denmark
- Austria
- Finland
- Sweden
- Italy
- Greece
- Spain
- Portugal
- or Eire

In theory, language is the only barrier.

Work outside the EU

Most European countries will accept foreign workers. However, the basis on which this occurs varies according to the country. Most of the non-EU countries in Europe will accept foreign workers only if the jobs they are taking cannot be carried out by a national of the country concerned. Work and residence permits, however, are required.

Although Norway is not currently an EU member it does allow EU citizens to take up a job there without a work permit. This is by virtue of the EEA (European Economic Area) agreement which Norway has with the EU countries.

Employment also divides into three distinct categories:

Executive and professional

Many people go abroad to follow or further a career. In this case you must have some specialist skill or profession to offer — for example, medicine or engineering — which will be sought after. On this basis executive and professional people may work in both EU and non-EU countries.

Casual employment

Many people, especially the young, go abroad as an experience, perhaps undertaking unskilled, casual work to pay for their travels, *ie* a working holiday. Usually, such work is only available legally in the EU. Non-EU countries in Europe do not usually permit foreigners to take casual work, in order to protect jobs for their own nationals.

Skilled/semi-skilled employment

It is rather harder to follow a trade or find semi-skilled work in Europe than either of the previous categories as few countries have any shortage in these areas. However, there is an absolute right for EU nationals to do this work in any EU country.

- Decide now: Which category do *you* fit into?

IS IT FOR ME?

Deciding to look for a job in Europe is a very personal matter. For some it seems a natural part of their career progression, whilst others do it for adventure. Yet others decide to make a whole new life for themselves.

A general principle is that working in Europe will not be for you unless you are prepared to take on the unpredictable. It is impossible to know whether you will find the job you want — or any job. It is difficult to say if it will be in a specific town, or even a specific country. You must be prepared to make the best of every situation. Even the very well qualified cannot afford to be too selective. If you do you will filter out too many opportunities.

The evidence is quite encouraging. Of the people who do go to live and work abroad very few (only about five per cent) return sooner than anticipated, having found the experience a total disaster. Most manage to adapt to and enjoy their situation. By the same token, though, not everyone stays working in Europe for good. A fair number of people work on fixed-term contracts of one, three or five years and then return to the UK. Only with the creation of the Single European Market are we starting to see more permanent migration within Europe.

THE LANGUAGE QUESTION

Although there is now free access to most jobs throughout the EU the language barrier still remains. Although language education almost everywhere is improving, each country will naturally continue to conduct business in its own national language. Contrary to popular belief in the UK, English is not widely spoken in most European countries. English may be the most widely used and understood language in the developed world, but it is a mistake for a UK national to rely on this if he or she is serious about working elsewhere in Europe. To make a success of working in Europe you will really need to either speak a European language, or be prepared to learn to a good basic standard. In most cases the effort will be worthwhile as you then have much greater access to jobs throughout Europe.

It needn't be as daunting as it sounds! There are lots of courses available for absolute beginners, as well as for those who want to brush up their existing knowledge. Some basic tips:

- get yourself a good basic language dictionary and use it regularly
- enrol on an intensive language course as soon as possible, and start speaking and writing the language as much as you can
- get some audio tapes and play them at home — or in the car
- tune in to a foreign language station on your radio
- if you have satellite TV, start watching some European programmes
- start taking a foreign language newspaper or magazine regularly
- make friends with as many European nationals as you can, for conversation and correspondence — conversation is especially helpful
- keep a special notebook or folder to collect as many words and phrases as you can to do with your chosen career.

Questions to ask yourself

- Do I like the UK too much to emigrate permanently?
- Do I really like foreign countries, other than for holidays?
- Am I prepared to learn a language?
- Am I a committed European, or is it just *one* country I have an affinity with?
- Do I have a definite skill to offer or not?
- If I hate working in Europe (or at the end of my contract) what will I do once back in the UK? Will I lose my place on the career ladder?

There are no right or wrong answers, but your honest replies to these questions will help you decide if you should go.

THE PROS AND CONS OF WORKING IN EUROPE

The pros

- Greater range of vacancies. Unemployment less of a problem in some countries.
- Most countries pay higher wages than the UK.
- Some careers carry more prestige in Europe, *eg* teaching.
- Some skills are more in demand in other countries, and the opportunities for promotion are better.
- The pace of work is more relaxed in some countries.
- Living costs and taxation are lower in some places giving you more disposable income.
- Your experience of working in Europe may make you a more desirable employee once back in the UK.

The cons

- The language barrier is a problem in *every* European country, except Eire. You will need to know or learn a foreign language.
- Some regions of Europe have severe unemployment.
- Locals tend to be favoured in most places, even in the EU where other EU nationals have an equal right to the jobs.
- National academic standards and training still differ.
- The pressure of work is more hectic in some parts of Europe, and/or conditions of work less pleasant.
- Rates of taxation (especially social security contributions) are higher than the UK in some places.

Fig. 1. The countries of Europe.

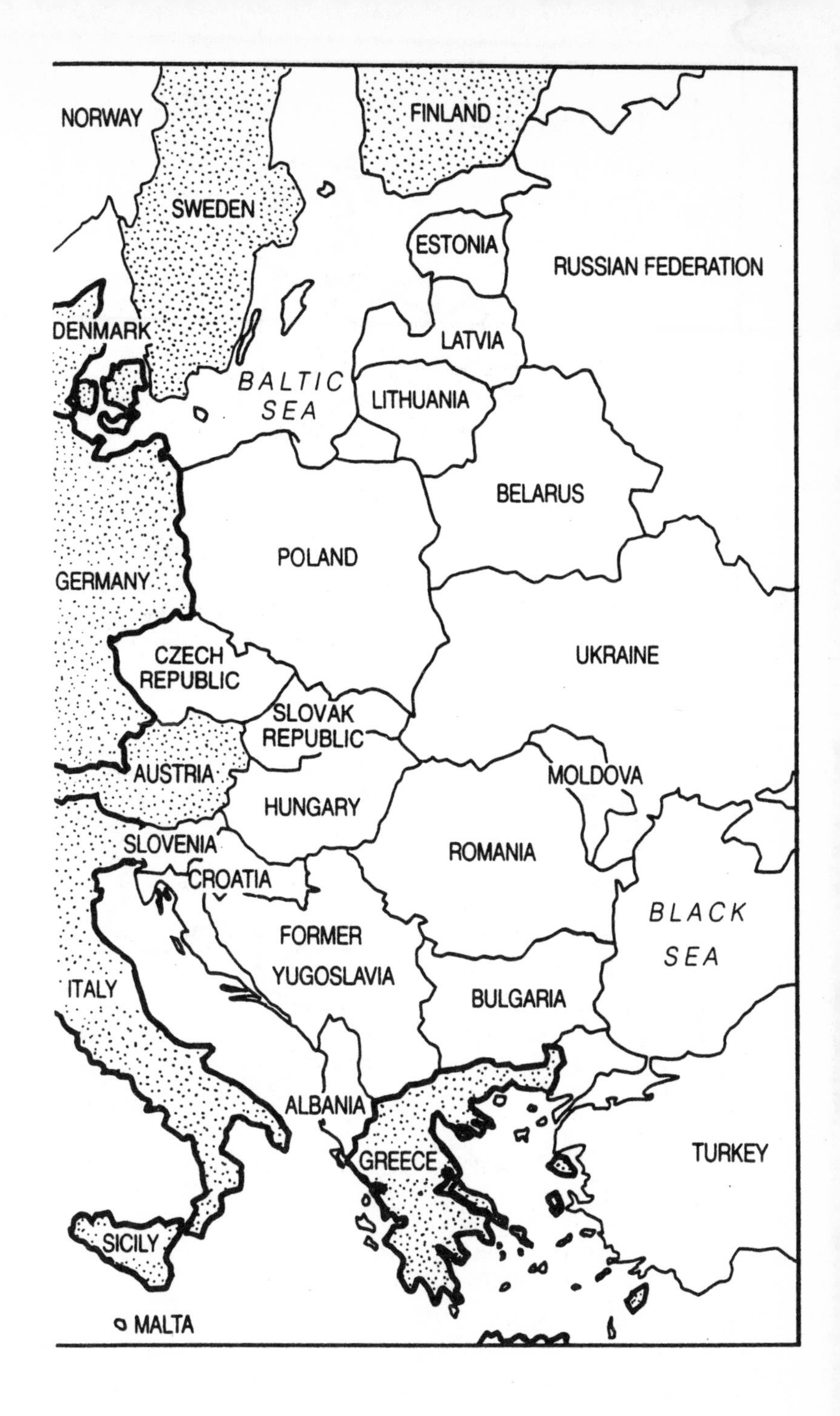
NORWAY
FINLAND
SWEDEN
ESTONIA
RUSSIAN FEDERATION
DENMARK
LATVIA
BALTIC SEA
LITHUANIA
BELARUS
POLAND
GERMANY
CZECH REPUBLIC
UKRAINE
SLOVAK REPUBLIC
AUSTRIA
MOLDOVA
HUNGARY
SLOVENIA
ROMANIA
CROATIA
BLACK SEA
FORMER YUGOSLAVIA
ITALY
BULGARIA
ALBANIA
GREECE
TURKEY
SICILY
MALTA

THE EUROPEAN UNION

Fact File

- The European Union (EU) was founded as the European Community in 1957 with the signing of the **Treaty of Rome**. The UK joined in 1973 and the 15 members are now France, Germany, Belgium, Netherlands, Luxembourg, Denmark, Italy, Greece, Spain, Portugal, Eire, United Kingdom, Austria, Sweden and Finland.
- The basic provisions of the Treaty of Rome were intended to remove all barriers to the free movement of people, capital, goods, services.
- The EU is not regarded as a single country. All 15 members are still **independent sovereign states**.
- The EU does not share a universal economic system.
- The EU does not share a universal system of government or politics.
- The EU does not have a universal law. Laws in every EU country are the responsibility of each individual government.
- The EU can, though, create laws and force members to adopt them.
- The EU countries do now have universal standards for many things, such as product standards, qualifications etc.
- The EU countries do not share tastes, customs and language.
- Nationals of one EU country have a right to live and work in any other EU country.
- Nationals of one EU country living in another are **resident aliens**, not **citizens** of that country. They *do not* share all the rights and obligations of nationals, but *do* so far as employment is concerned.

Fig. 2. Fact file on the European Union.

PERSONAL ACTION PLAN I

The size of the EU alone — 360 million consumers — makes it very important to plan ahead as much as possible. It is essential to have some definite aims, otherwise you may find you are presented with too many opportunities, none of which is suitable. Even worse is the danger of signing a contract taking you into a totally unsuitable job.

The best general advice is to be single-minded but flexible. Be prepared to consider different options critically. You might, for example, be a salesman or woman with the desire and commitment to make a success of selling cars in the Côte d'Azur. But it is as well to have some secondary, related aims in mind — such as selling packaging machinery in Provence, or moving into the motor trade in Murcia, Spain. After all, the Single European Market is aimed at promoting competition and flexibility in business, and achieving that requires everyone to be flexible.

The following action plan should help to order your thoughts:

1. Decide which job or jobs you ideally want. If possible this should be something you are skilled and/or qualified in.

2. Decide which country or countries you would most like to live and work in. Which European language do you know best or could you learn most easily?

3. Find out where the industries needing your type of job are located (see Chapter 5).

4. Cross-reference the countries listed at 2 and 3 above to find the optimum European country for you.

5. Start to look for vacancies in the optimum country. Information on this is given in Chapter 2. Initially, do this whilst based at home in the UK.

6. If insufficient vacancies are identified this way then consider visiting the country to look for work, where permitted (see Chapter 2).

7. Build up a network of possible jobs and possible countries. Make as many applications as possible. Do not depend on just one or two.

8. Select and accept the most promising job!

SOME TYPICAL CASE HISTORIES

Andrew Smith

Age:	27
UK location:	Bristol
Trade/profession:	Motor engineer
Qualifications:	GCSE and vocational qualifications. Speaks basic German
Wanted to move to:	Germany
Wanted to do:	Motor engineering, BMW/Mercedes factory
Eventually moved to:	Bavaria, Germany
Eventually did:	Technician, BMW dealership
Pay/conditions:	DM59,600/year, permanent contract

John Wood

Age:	39
UK location:	East Yorkshire
Trade/profession:	Systems analyst
Qualifications:	Degree
Wanted to move to:	Eastern Europe
Wanted to do:	Work for computer company
Eventually moved to:	Helsinki, Finland
Eventually did:	Works for computer company expanding into eastern European market but based in Finland
Pay/conditions:	Three year contract. £40,000 reviewed after 12 months

Marion Churchill

Age:	23
UK location:	Dorset
Trade/profession:	Personal assistant (PA)
Qualifications:	GCSE and 'A' levels. Fluent in French
Wanted to move to:	Brussels
Wanted to do:	Work for European Commission
Eventually moved to:	Nancy, France
Eventually did:	PA to export director
Pay/conditions:	FF160,000/year plus health benefits, permanent contract

Michael Lister

Age:	18
UK location:	West Yorkshire
Trade/profession:	Student, taking year off before university
Qualifications:	GCSEs and 'A' levels. No specialist language knowledge
Wanted to move to:	France or Spain
Wanted to do:	Any casual work
Eventually moved to:	Magaluf, Majorca
Eventually did:	Work in bar and leaflet dropping (four months)
Pay/conditions:	PTAS450/hour, no contract

Yvonne Carlton

Age:	42
UK location:	Coventry
Trade/profession:	Housewife, some secretarial experience
Qualifications:	'O' levels
Wanted to move to:	Moved to Madrid with husband on executive posting. (Took evening class course in Spanish.)
Wanted to do:	Any part time work
Eventually moved to:	Madrid
Eventually did:	Language teaching assistant at private English language school
Pay/conditions:	PTAS1,400/hour, 20 hours per week, renewable 12-month contract

These examples show the diversity of both opportunities and people now working in Europe, and support the feeling that the job and place you might want is not always what you will eventually get and be perfectly happy doing.

2

How Do You Find a Job in Europe?

In many ways the European job finding network is already quite well established; the sources of a job in Europe are much the same as the sources of a job at home. All the various sources of jobs are discussed here. If anything, there are too many different sources of jobs in Europe than too few. By and large, though, a process of trial and error must be used. Try them all and see what happens.

USING THE MEDIA

UK newspapers

Many newspapers now have European job advertisements in their 'Situations' columns. At present these tend to be executive and professional vacancies only, but a small number of skilled/semi-skilled vacancies are starting to appear. The most useful UK newspapers to use are the national quality dailies, rather than the tabloid or regional newspapers. In any one week these newspapers can be relied upon to provide between 40 and 60 European vacancies. Publications to try include:

Daily Telegraph (pools some recruitment advertising with France's *Le Figaro* and Spain's *La Vanguardia*)
Sunday Telegraph
Financial Times
Daily Mail
Daily Express
Mail on Sunday
Sunday Express
Independent
Guardian
Times
Independent on Sunday
Sunday Times

Currently the progress of newspapers published on a Europe-wide scale has been slow and one attempt to do this with *The European* newspaper was eventually closed down.

Before subscribing to specific newspapers make a list of those which are most appropriate to your trade or profession at the reading room of a main library. Most newspapers nominate one day for recruitment advertising, or specialise in different professions each day.

If the advertisement is in English this tends to suggest that the employer is seeking an English speaking applicant.

European newspapers

UK job seekers are just as entitled to use European newspapers as nationals of the respective countries. However, there are two fundamental problems:

- The language barrier: can you understand the publication?
- The language barrier: if the advertisement is in a foreign language you probably need to speak that language to carry out the job.

The main foreign newspapers, such as France's *France-Soir* and Germany's *Frankfurter Allgemeine* are available the day after publication at large newsagents in the UK. UK prices are high compared with the cover price. If you wish to subscribe to these or other European newspapers then the embassy of the relevant country will often let you have a contact address.

Some European countries have English language newspapers, including the *Athens News* or Brussels' *The Bulletin*. Where they do exist they are an excellent source of jobs, but usually only for casual work.

Which magazines, journals and bulletins to use

Magazines and journals

Magazines and journals have always been a good source of international vacancies. Consider trade and professional magazines, rather than general interest ones. UK magazines and journals have long contained international vacancies, just as those in mainland Europe also include vacancies in different parts of the world.

Such magazines are only a source of professional and executive vacancies, but some of them are published in English which suggests it is not necessary to speak the local language to apply for the job in question. For example, *Flight International* magazine is published in the UK but is a world authority on its subject and includes vacancies all around the world.

It is worth making the most complete list you can of what magazines and journals apply to your particular trade or profession:

- UK magazines can be located by looking in *Benn's Media Directory*.
- International magazines can be located in *Benn's Media Directory International.*

Specialist bulletins
Some countries have special vacancy journals or bulletins which list vacancies, usually executive and professional ones only. For example, France has *Courier Cadre* and Germany has *Markt+Chance* (see Chapter 5).

In the UK there are some specialist publications for those looking for work overseas or already working overseas. The main ones are:

- *Home and Away*
- *Overseas Jobs Express.*

Details are given in the Further Information section.

THE UK EMPLOYMENT SERVICE

It is possible to use the UK national Employment Service in order to find vacancies which have been notified to the state employment services in other EU countries. Links are now well established by way of the EURES (European Employment Services) network so that you can find out about jobs in Europe at your local Job Centre.

In the UK the system is operated by the Overseas Placing Unit (OPU) of the Employment Service in Sheffield. However, details of actual vacancies in Europe and general information about working in EU countries are available via the NATVACS system at your local Job Centre. Some of the jobs are also listed on the ES Jobfinder service on Channel 4 Teletext p.649.

If you find a suitable job by either of these methods you can apply for it using form ES13 available at Job Centres.

In addition, there are Euroadvisers working in selected cities around the UK. These Euroadvisers deal with more complicated enquiries about working in Europe and can also help you with an application for a particular job. A list of Euroadvisers is given on page 26.

Limitations

It is important to realise that the EURES system is not a pan-European job agency as such; rather it is a system for exchanging information about vacancies and available personnel across Europe. These are usually selected vacancies, often ones that are difficult to fill locally.

The system is best suited to those who have a sought after skill or experience to offer. Even then the chances of being offered a job from a speculative application are minimal. It can rarely help the unskilled or semi-skilled. It is essential to have language ability in the country in question and the OPU cannot help with arranging interviews, contracts and permits.

In addition to the EU countries Norway participates in EURES.

- The Employment Service, Overseas Placing Unit (OPU), Rockingham House, 123 West Street, Sheffield S1 4ER. Tel: (0114) 259 6051.

European state employment services

Any EU national is entitled to use the state employment service in any other EU country. Foreigners are not usually allowed to use employment services in non-EU countries, although there are some exceptions. EU employment services are obliged to give EU nationals the same treatment as any national. In practice some do and some do not. In any case you need to be able to speak the local language to deal with them, and to take the jobs they have available.

Foreign employment services will not usually deal with telephoned or written enquiries from abroad. You can try but would need to be fluent in the local language. Better service is usually received if you can deal with the Job Centre in person.

Addresses of state employment services can be obtained from:

- The London embassy of the country in question.
- The national telephone directory of the country.

Special tip: the OPU and EURES network does not provide access to all vacancies in *all* EU countries. Many more vacancies are available by contacting the state employment service direct.

USING PRIVATE EMPLOYMENT AGENCIES

UK agencies

An increasing number of private employment agencies in the UK are now starting to handle vacancies in European countries, although it is

United Kingdom Euroadvisers

Employment Service
Overseas Placing Unit
Rockingham House
123 West Street
Sheffield S1 4ER.
Tel: (0114) 259 6086/6089
Fax: (0114) 259 6040

Training & Employment Agency
Gloucester House
Chichester Street
Belfast BT1 4RA.
Tel: (028) 9025 2141
Fax: (028) 9025 2288

Employment Service
Northern Region (EIU)
5th Floor
Broadacre House
Market Street
Newcastle on Tyne
NE1 6HQ.
Tel: (0191) 211 4420
Fax: (0191) 211 4405

Employment Service
Office for Wales (EIU)
Companies House
Crown Way
Cardiff CF4 3UW.
Tel: (029) 2038 0781
Fax: (029) 2034 3944

Employment Service
South West Region (EIU)
6th floor
The Pithay
Bristol BS1 2NQ.
Tel: (0117) 945 6730
Fax: (0117) 945 96960

Employment Service
Yorks & Humber Region (EIU)
Jubilee House
33-41 Park Place
Leeds LS1 2RE.
Tel: (0113) 245 9546
Fax: (0113) 245 3574

Employment Service
West Midlands Region (EIU)
2 Duchess Place
Hagley Road
Birmingham
B16 8NS.
Tel: (0121) 452 5410
Fax: (0121) 452 5431

Employment Service
Edinburgh Jobcentre
11–13 South Andrew Street
Edinburgh
EH2 2BT
Tel: (0131) 456 3359
Fax: (0131) 456 3325

Employment Service
Hammersmith Jobcentre
Glen House
22 Glenthorne Road
London
W6 0PP
Tel: (020) 8210 8184
Fax: (020) 8210 8181

Employment Service
East Midlands & Eastern
Newton House
Maid Marion Way
Nottingham NG1 6GG
Tel: (0115) 989 5912
Fax: (0115) 989 5707

Fig. 3. United Kingdom Euroadvisers.

still only a fraction of all those in operation. Usually, agencies are retained by the employer to fill a vacancy with a suitable applicant, rather than offering to find a job for a job-seeker. However, it is still worth contacting them to see if vacancies are available; some agencies will register your details for three to six months in case something suitable becomes available.

Most agencies deal in specific countries and specific industries only, rather than all vacancies across the board. Suitable agencies can be located:

- In the UK *Yellow Pages*. Look under Employment Agencies and Consultants.

- In the Yearbook of the Federation of Recruitment and Employment Services Ltd (FRES). Their address is 36-38 Mortimer Street, London W1N 7RB.

- In the *CEPEC Recruitment Guide*, available at main libraries. (Mostly of use to executives and professionals.)

European agencies

There is no reason why you cannot use private employment agencies in your chosen destination country. Sometimes there will be a language barrier but agencies in some countries, especially the Netherlands, are already well equipped to deal with enquiries from overseas.

The role of private agencies varies across Europe. In some countries (like the Netherlands) such agencies thrive. In others (like Germany) they are largely forbidden. In others (like France) private agencies are limited to handling only temporary vacancies.

Most agencies will be reputable but it is worth proceeding with caution and reconsidering ones that ask for fees. Agencies are usually paid by the employer, but in a few places the agency becomes your employer and pays your wages, which are less than that paid by the actual employer.

Agencies can be dealt with from the UK, especially for more professional/executive vacancies. However, it is better to deal with them in person. Suitable agencies can be located by two methods:

- Their own advertisements in foreign newspapers.
- The *Yellow Pages* of the country in question. These are often available at main libraries in the UK.

Jane C. James
1 The Road
Anytown
Lancashire LA1 1AA
England
+ 44 0123 999999
1 February XXXX

Kölner Gmbh
Breite Str. 223
D-5000 Köln
Germany

Dear Sirs,

I am writing to introduce myself and enquire whether you might have any vacancies for secretaries or administrative staff with your company.

I am 22 years of age and currently employed as a secretary with an engineering company in England. I am fully experienced in all aspects of secretarial work including shorthand, typing, wordprocessing, computer operation and general administration. In addition to being an English speaker I speak some German and I am currently undertaking a part-time course in written German at Anytown College.

I am particularly interested in securing a position in Köln and feel that there would be many benefits in employing an English speaking secretary for a company, like Kölner, which trades with the UK. I enclose a copy of my latest CV* which gives full details of my qualifications and career to date.

If you have any vacancies, either now or in the future, for which I might be suitable, then please do not hesitate to contact me further so that we may discuss the possibilities.

Yours faithfully,

Jane James

*enclosing a copy of your CV with such a letter will make your speculative application clearer and more concise (see Chapter 3).

Fig. 4. Approaching a company by letter.

THE ART OF WRITING LETTERS

Not all jobs, and especially those abroad, are found by replying to advertised vacancies. A fair proportion are obtained by what might be called **speculative application**. That is, by approaching potential employers and offering your services. Chances of being offered a job immediately are slim but it does happen and, even if not successful immediately, it is a good way of building up contacts for future use.

There are frequent examples of this method being successful. One job seeker secured a job in an Italian vineyard by writing to an address in a good wine guide. Another found work with the car manufacturer BMW, simply by writing to BMW, München, Germany. The comparatively small cost of paper and postage means that it is invariably worth trying, whilst also bearing in mind the limitations.

Prepare a suitable letter, outlining yourself and your experience. Then, make a mailing list of companies who operate in the industry to which your particular skills and qualifications relate. A mailing campaign can then be started, writing to as many of the addresses as possible. Access to a wordprocessor will make this method much more practical.

Company addresses can be obtained from various sources:

- European newspapers
- European magazines and journals
- *Yellow Pages* directory of the respective country, which should be available at main libraries in the UK
- Trade directories from the respective country, often available in UK libraries: for example, the *Kompass* series of guides.

The sample letter in Figure 4 could be adapted for your use, and written in the appropriate language.

ADVERTISING IN NEWSPAPERS FOR 'SITUATIONS WANTED'

An alternative to writing letters in a speculative search for work is to place a Situations Wanted advertisement in newspapers in the country in question. Much depends on the country, circulation and type of work you are seeking but it can work. Details of some newspapers to advertise in are given in Chapter 5.

What should you say?

In most cases, advertising rates are high, so the shorter and punchier your advertisement the better. If possible, keep to under 20 words. You should say:

- who you are
- what you can do
- what qualifications or experience you have
- where to contact you.

Figure 5 shows an example of this.

> **English girl**. Age 21. Seeks nannying position with happy family in Amsterdam. 8-12 months. Lots of experience with babies and children. Driving licence. Willing to do housework. Phone: 0000000.

Fig. 5. How to advertise yourself.

Unless you know the local language it can be worth writing in English. Of course, fewer people will be able to respond but it will stand out and, of course, you might not be able to work with those who cannot speak English anyway.

How do you place an advertisement?

Some major European newspapers can now accept advertisement bookings from the UK by phone or fax and take credit card payment. If you have difficulty with this then an advertising agent can take care of all this for you. They can advise on where to advertise, make bookings, and accept payment in UK currency. One of the main agents is:

Powers International Ltd
100 Rochester Row
London SW1P 1JP.
Tel: (020) 7630 9966
Fax: (020) 7630 9922

Payment is usually required in advance and 10-14 days' notice is needed.

Depending on which area you wish to work in, choose a local, regional or national newspaper. Local newspapers are better for casual work, national ones are better for skilled jobs. Some European countries have no or few national newspapers; in France the regional press is more important and hardly any newspapers circulate nationally.

MAKING USE OF PROFESSIONAL ASSOCIATIONS

A little known source of help in finding a job is to seek help from any professional associations you may be a member of, or which you might be able to join. These organisations can often suggest European employment contacts, or suggest their counterpart in the respective country which might help. Alternatively, they may be able to give you a letter of introduction. Try:

- professional bodies
- trades unions
- trade/employers' bodies.

A useful source of contacts is *Trade Unions and Professional Bodies of the UK*. Also refer to the *Directory of British Associations*, *Directory of European Associations* and *Directory of Pan-European Associations*. These are published by CBD Research Publications and are at main libraries.

EMBASSIES AND CHAMBERS OF COMMERCE

Embassies, consulates and chambers of commerce are not official sources of employment information, but they are a direct link to the country and may be approached for current information and advice. Some will refuse to reply, whereas others are quite helpful. They may supply:

- addresses of state employment agencies
- addresses of some private employment agencies
- details of trade directories containing addresses
- details of national newspapers
- photocopies of *Yellow Pages* for their own country.

Do not expect to get details of actual vacancies (but you could ask). The main aim is to get contacts from which you can obtain addresses for speculative applications. Addresses of embassies are given in the Information section.

Chambers of commerce will either have a free list of member companies or a directory of member companies available to purchase.

3

How to Apply for a Job in Europe

Locating vacancies is a major step on the way to finding a job in Europe — but then comes the process of application.

National practices vary considerably, and this is one area where standardisation within the EU is only just starting to take effect.

No matter where you are applying — whether Madrid or Munich — competence, care and commitment in making the application rarely fail to impress in any language.

USING YOUR QUALIFICATIONS

It is only in the last few years that a significant number of UK qualifications have been accepted as valid in other EU countries, and vice versa. Over the last few years the **European Centre for the Development of Vocational Training** (CEDEFOP) in Berlin has been working to introduce systems by which many academic and most professional qualifications can be recognised in other countries.

Two systems are now in force; they are **Harmonised Training Directives** and the **First General System of Mutual Recognition of Qualifications**.

Harmonised Training Directives

Under the Harmonised Training system, CEDEFOP has examined training courses all over the EU and decided which can be deemed to offer largely the same programme of training. The qualifications this applies to include:

- doctors
- dentists
- nurses
- midwives
- vets

- architects
- pharmacists
- GPs
- and those in road transport.

The First General System of Mutual Recognition of Qualifications

Under this system training courses may have very different programmes, but the eventual qualification is considered of similar standard. The First System covers all qualifications obtained after three years' post secondary study, including university degrees, plus all lesser qualifications in certain fields most notably:

- manufacturing/processing industries
- food/beverage industries
- wholesale trades
- intermediaries in commerce and industry
- retail trade
- wholesale coal trade
- trade in toxic products
- hotel/catering
- insurance agents/brokers
- transport/travel agency
- hairdressing
- some fishery, postal and telecommunications, recreational, community and personal services.

More sectors may be added. The DTI and the Employment Department can provide further details.

Under EU directives those qualified to work in one profession in one EU state are usually qualified to undertake it in another. However, an employer is still entitled to expect you to be competent to do the work and to speak the local language adequately. In some circumstances you can be required to undertake an aptitude test or period of supervised training.

School qualifications

At the moment school qualifications are not usually officially recognised in other EU countries. This, however, may change in future when all school qualifications and qualifications such as NVQs (National Vocational Qualifications) may either be recognised or at least become considered as equivalent to local qualifications in each individual country.

Ask the DTI and the Employment Department for the latest details.

Is certification necessary?

It is not necessary to have your qualifications formally transferred to any other country. If appropriate they should be recognised as they stand. Further information can be obtained from:

The Comparability Co-Ordinator
Overseas Placing Unit
Level 3
Rockingham House
123 West Street
Sheffield
S1 4ER.
Tel: (0114) 259 6051

If you are abroad details of comparability can be obtained by asking the local office of the state employment service to make enquiries with that country's National Academic Recognition Information Centre (NARIC) on your behalf.

It is always worth detailing your qualifications when applying for a job in the EU. Qualifications from outside the EU, especially degrees, may not be officially recognised but may still be respected. Degrees from British universities are recognised by most countries as denoting a high standard of achievement.

USING YOUR EXPERIENCE

The **European Community Certificate of Experience** exists so that your experience can be recognised and used to get a job in an EU country. If you have at least three to five years' experience in a particular field (it is not necessary to be qualified) you may qualify for a document which certifies your experience.

Certificates are issued by the Department of Trade and Industry (DTI) in the UK. The process takes about four weeks. The issuing authority will look at your experience, which you should be able to prove, and at the relevant EU directives, and decide if you qualify for a certificate.

The trades which the Certificate of Experience currently covers are:

- manufacturing/processing industries
- retail trade

- wholesale trade
- wholesale coal trade
- hotel/catering
- transport/travel agency
- hairdressing
- some fishery, postal, telecommunications, recreational, community and personal services.

A Certificate of Experience can be useful where qualifications may be needed for a particular job in the EU but not in the UK. An example of this is hairdressing. The Certificate may be accepted instead. However, an employer will still expect you to be competent to do the work and to speak the local language.

Enquiries about, and applications for, the Certificate can be handled by:

Department of Trade and Industry (DTI)
Ashdown House
1 Victoria Street
London SW1H 0EZ.
Tel: (020) 7215 5000
Web: http://www.dti.gov.uk

HOW DO EUROPEANS RECRUIT?

Methods of recruitment

Despite the fact that qualifications and experience may be harmonised in the EU, the system of recruitment across Europe still varies according to national custom. Indeed, no other European country has systems of recruiting and vacancy filling that are as comprehensive as those in the UK.

Europe-wide there are four main methods of filling vacancies:

- Advertising. In newspapers or through agencies, etc.

- Headhunting. In some countries poaching staff is commonplace. It is difficult for a foreigner to tie into this system.

- Speculative application. Talking yourself into a job. Personal contacts and rapport count for so much in every mainland European country.

- Word of mouth. In some countries (principally Spain, Portugal,

Sample Certificate of Experience

....
(authority or competent body) (place)

CERTIFICATE

as to activities pursued under the provisions of the Directives adopted by the Council of the European Communities laying down detailed provisions for transitional measures in the field of freedom of establishment and freedom to provide services

Mr
Mrs ....
Miss (name, forenames)

born on ....at ....

nationality ....

permanent address ....

(A) has produced evidence showing that he/she worked

1. in a self-employed capacity

   from ....to ....

   name and address of undertaking ....

   ....

   description of undertaking ....

   ....

   from ....to ....

   name and address of undertaking ....

   ....

   description of undertaking ....

   ....

2. as manager of an undertaking or of a branch thereof

   ....

   from ....to ....

   name and address of undertaking or branch

   ....

   description of undertaking or branch ....

   ....

years	months

Fig. 6. The EC Certificate of Experience (continued overleaf).

from .... to ....

name and address of undertaking or branch ....

....

description of undertaking or branch ....

....

3. as deputy to the proprietor or to the manager of an undertaking

from .... to ....

name and address of undertaking ....

....

description of undertaking ....

....

from .... to ....

name and address of undertaking ....

....

description of undertaking ....

....

years	months

4. in a managerial post
(i) with duties of a technical nature
(ii) with duties of commercial nature
(iii) with duties of a type normally pertaining to the occupation in question and with responsibilities for one or more departments of the undertaking
from..to ....
name and address of undertaking ....
....
description of undertaking ....
....
from..to ....
name and address of undertaking ....
....
description of undertaking ....
....

5. in an employed capacity
from..to ....
name and address of undertaking ....
....
description of undertaking ....
....
from..to ....
name and address of undertaking ....
....
description of undertaking ....
....

years	months

(B) has provided evidence showing that between ....and ....
he/she followed a course of training as a ....
and that he/she completed such training by obtaining [name of officially recognized certificate or diploma] ....
....

name of issuing body...
or that such training is regarded by [competent professional body] ....
....

as fully satisfying its requirements.

This certificate constitutes proof to the competent authorities of the Member States of the European Communities of the training received of the activities pursued and should be submitted in support of application for any authorization required under the law of the host country to pursue any of the activities of self-employed persons covered by the relevant Directives.

Date ....

Stamp/Signature

(To be completed only in respect of activities for which there exists an official occupation description in the host country.)

Details of activities pursued

1. Description of occupation in host country ....

....

2. Name, description and address of undertaking (where appropriate indicate also the function of the department concerned)

....
....
....
....
....
....
....
....
....
....
....
....

Exact description of the activities pursued (in accordance with the occupation description in the host country as set out in the list compiled by the Commission of the European Communities, using as far as possible the figures given therein)

....
....
....
....
....
....
....
....
....
....
....
....

Greece and Italy) most jobs are found by a system of networking and contacts. It helps to be on the spot to use this method.

What are the employer's expectations?

Employers in different parts of Europe have different expectations of their potential employees. British employers, for example, tend to place great emphasis on basic school qualifications, experience and an unbroken ladder of career progression. This is not always the case elsewhere. Factors which can be taken into consideration include:

- Elitism. In most countries some schools/universities have much more sway than others. This is especially true in France.

- Professionalism. Trade and professional qualifications are more respected in other European countries than the UK. Exam certificates mean everything in most of them.

- Status. Some countries, even republican states like France, place great emphasis on family status, past and present.

- Contacts. In some countries the right contacts are needed to get many jobs. This applies especially in Spain, Italy and Greece. In Britain we may call it nepotism but it is part and parcel of recruitment in many countries.

The overall message here is to be sure to prepare your application with particular thought, and recognise that both methods and the importance of particular qualities will always vary nationally, Single European Market or not.

WRITING A LETTER OF APPLICATION

What language should you write in?

The first consideration is whether to write in the local language, or in English. Basic English is sometimes understood as a business language in all European countries but this should not be taken for granted. In addition, in most European countries those who can speak English may speak our language much better than they can read it. Some nationalities, especially the French, feel passionately about their own language and tend to avoid using foreign languages (like English) even if their command of them is good.

Writing in English creates the risk that the reader will not be able to understand you. On the other hand it may commend you to them as a native speaker of English. Generally, there is no advantage in using a translator to write in the local language if this would suggest your language ability is better than it is. Weigh up each situation individually and try to come to the best compromise possible.

How to write for a European reader

The keynote when writing letters overseas is simplicity. Even the foreign reader who speaks some English is rarely as familiar with the language as you. Really think about every word you write: its colloquial meaning to you may be totally different to the dictionary meaning which the foreign reader will probably understand.

Style

Style should generally be quite formal; few European countries are as relaxed in business as the UK. Take care with titles and forms of address. Do not use first names. Splitting the letter down into paragraphs of just one point is a good way to make a letter clearer.

Length

Ideally do not exceed two A4 pages for a letter of application. If you are also enclosing a CV (curriculum vitae) then one A4 page should be appropriate.

Content

The secret with a letter is to say everything you wish to say but in the shortest possible format. A good, quick method is to devote a paragraph to each important point, as follows:

- What job are you applying for and where did you see it advertised?
- Why is this a job you feel you *have to* apply for?
- How are you qualified for this job?
- What experience do you have that will be useful?
- Write yourself a testimonial! Explain what job you do now and give an example of your value to your employer.
- Commitment. Re-affirm your interest in the job.
- Invite further queries from the employer, or request an interview.

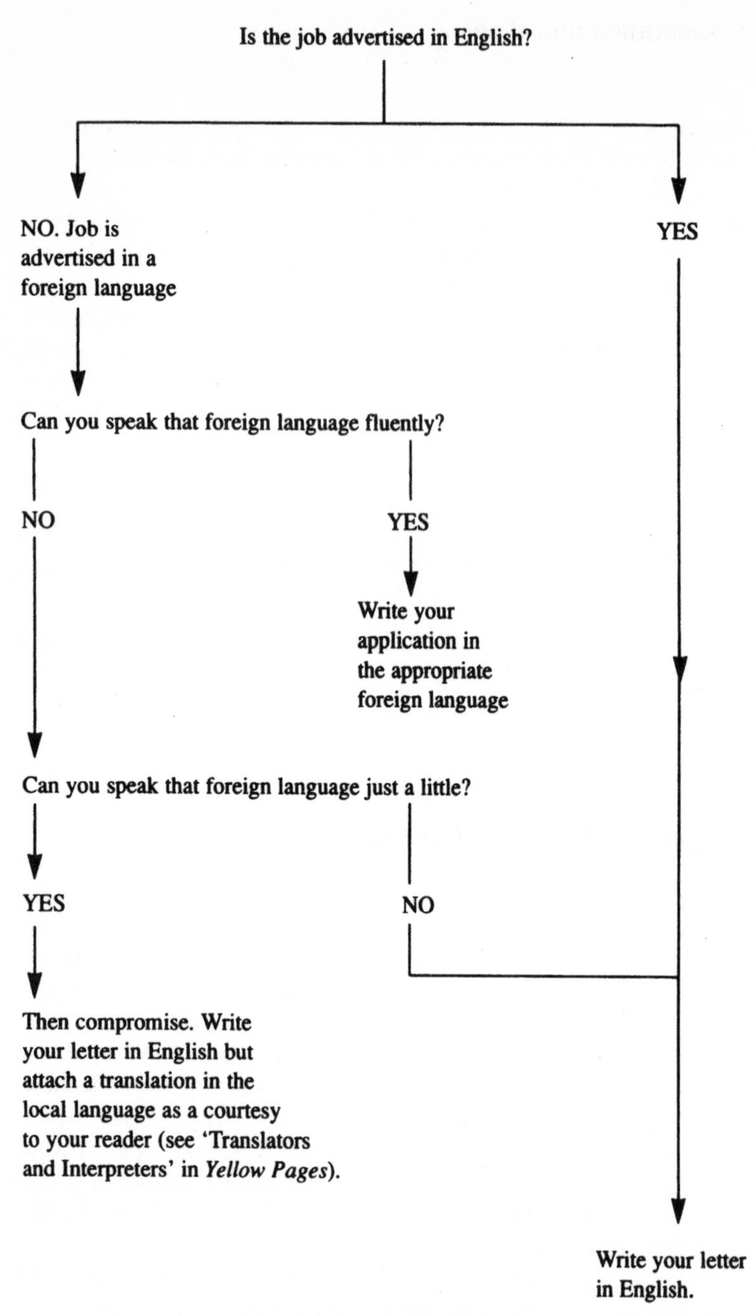

Fig. 7. Breaking down the language barrier.

Presentation guidelines

Letters of application should always be well presented. Standards of presentation are important in every country. No country in Europe is as relaxed or informal in this respect as the UK. Most are comparatively old-fashioned; 'flashiness' in a business letter is rarely appreciated. Also:

- Always type your letter if possible; if not because this is expected, then for clarity. A doubled-spaced letter will allow the reader to pencil in queries or translations.

- Quote your country name in the address.

- Always quote a telephone contact if possible. Quote your telephone number internationally. For example:
  + 44 161 999999
  '+' indicates the caller's international code. '44' is the UK international code. Quote your number without '0' of the STD code; *eg* 161 indicates Manchester.

- Avoid abbreviations that may be confusing. Explain what qualifications (*eg* BSc, BA) mean.

- Staple pages of a letter together. A foreign reader may not easily be able to see which follows on from which.

HOW DO YOU FILL IN FORMS?

All the European countries have a much greater liking for bureaucracy than the UK, and form-filling is a national pastime in Germany, France and Italy especially. This can pose a problem due both to language difficulties and the fact that information requested is not always the same as that in the UK.

Some countries use multilingual application forms but there is no standard European form in general use. Generally, there is a tendency for forms to be shorter than is now customary in the UK, but they are structured differently and ask for details that a British employer would not normally want to know. For example, in many countries, it is usual to request a photograph to be attached, so a supply of passport photographs can be useful.

The specimen form in Figure 8 is similar to that used by the Commission of the European Communities and other large

APPLICATION FORM

Please attach a
recent passport photo
here

1.

SURNAME: FIRST NAME: SECOND NAME: MAIDEN NAME:

....

2. **PLACE OF BIRTH:** ....

DATE OF BIRTH: ....

NATIONALITY AT BIRTH: ....

PRESENT NATIONALITY: ....

Fig. 8. Sample European application form.

3. SECONDARY EDUCATION:

Name and location of establishment	Exact dates attended	Diplomas or Degrees obtained	Main subjects	Marks
....	....	....	....	....
....	....	....	....	....
....	....	....	....	....
....	....	....	....	....

4. MOTHER TONGUE: ....

OTHER LANGUAGES: ....

State level of knowledge: V.Good/Good/Fair

5. POST APPLIED FOR: ....

6. EXPLAIN BRIEFLY WHY YOU ARE INTERESTED IN THIS POST

....

....

....

7. ADDRESS FOR CORRESPONDENCE:

....

....

Tel: ....

8. PERMANENT ADDRESS: ....

....

Tel: ....

9. SEX: ....

10. MARITAL STATUS: ....

11. HAVE YOU ANY DEPENDANTS? Yes/No

DETAILS

Name	Date of birth	Relationship
....	....	....
....	....	....
....	....	....

12. PREVIOUS EMPLOYMENT:

Employer's name	From/to	Nature of work	Salary
....	....	....	....
....	....	....	....

13. REFERENCES:

Please give the names and addresses of three persons (not relatives) who will provide a character reference. At least one should know your qualifications.

Full name	Full address	Profession
....	....	....
....	....	....
....	....	....

14. FURTHER INFORMATION WITH WHICH YOU WISH TO SUPPORT YOUR APPLICATION:

....

....

....

15. HOW DID YOU LEARN OF THIS VACANCY?

....

DECLARATION:

I the undersigned declare that the above information is true and complete. I understand that any false statement or omission may lead to dismissal.

Signed: .... Date: ....

organisations. It illustrates the type of form you might expect to have to fill in. It may be a good idea to complete this specimen now so that all the information is to hand when you have actual forms to complete.

PREPARING A EURO-CV

In common with the UK, most countries of Europe are familiar with the use of the CV (curriculum vitae), or biography as it may be known. In the central European countries and Scandinavia it is considered virtually obligatory for all but manual and unskilled workers to have some form of CV. In other places, such as Spain, Greece and Portugal it is a fairly new concept and considered something of a fashionable accessory.

How to prepare a CV

A CV should always be a statement of information: that is, basic information. A CV is not the place for a 'hard sell' to an employer — a letter of application is more appropriate for 'selling' yourself. A CV for European use should be as simple as possible, thus avoiding misunderstandings. Avoid the use of abbreviations and explain terms (*eg* BSc, BA) that may not be understood in other countries.

Checklist

You should include:

- your full name
- clear contact address and telephone
- school qualifications
- post school qualifications
- clear contact addresses for referees
- work history, including details of responsibilities
- interests/qualifications not connected with work.

How to present a CV

A CV should occupy no more than a single A4 page. This will make it easy to read, and it will illustrate your ability to present information concisely. Always type your CV; there is really no such thing as a handwritten CV. It is quite satisfactory to have a good quality photocopied one or even a professionally printed one.

The model CV for Europe

The format for CVs varies over Europe and it is difficult to identify a standard one. However, Figure 9 shows a model CV for Europe which would be broadly acceptable in most European countries. You may wish to prepare your own CV along these lines.

This CV form has been prepared so as to keep language problems to a minimum. It is worded in English, French, German, Spanish and Italian respectively. These five key languages are either the main language or quite widely understood in most European countries. Your CV prepared just once in this format will suffice for use all over Europe.

DEALING WITH INTERVIEWS

Whether to travel or not?

Hopefully, the eventual result of your application will be the offer of an interview. Then, it is necessary to decide if you'll go. An interview might be in the UK, or you may have to cross the Channel to attend one.

- Was the job advertised in the UK? Then you can almost certainly expect an interview to be arranged in the UK, perhaps by a UK-based agent or recruitment consultancy.

- Was the job advertised in the appropriate country? Then it is unlikely that interviews will be held in the UK.

If you are asked to travel overseas to an interview, you may have to bear the cost and you should consider whether it is likely to be worthwhile. This is a matter only you can decide, but as a general rule:

- If the job is unskilled/semi-skilled: travel expenses will not usually be paid.

- If the job is skilled: a contribution *may* be offered.

- If the job is executive/professional — salary over £50,000 or thereabouts — you can probably expect full travel expenses to be offered.

Preparing for interview

You should prepare for an interview before leaving the UK. Various information, forms and documents may be required and these can only be obtained at home. In addition it is much easier, and often cheaper too, to take things from home rather than get them in a foreign country. You might take:

CURRICULUM VITAE

Name/Nom/Name/Apellidos/Nome:

Address/Adresse/Anschrift/Dirección/Indirizzo:

Tel:

Date of birth/Date de naissance/Geburtsdatum/Fecha de nacimiento/Data di nascita:

Nationality/Nationalité/Staatsangehörigkeit/Nacionalidad/ Cittadinanza:

Education/Etudes/Ausbildungagang/Estudios/Studi:

Work experience/Expérience professionelle/ Berufserfahrung/Experiencia profesional/Esperienza professionale:

Fig. 9. A model CV for Europe.

Reference/Référence/Referenz/Referencia/Referenza (Attestąto)	
1.	2.

Interests outside work/Activités extra-professionelles/ Ausserberufliche/Actividades extra-profesionales/ Attività o attitudini extraprofessionali:

Other information/Information supplémentaire/Zusätzlich information/Información adicional/Informazioni supplementare:

Date/Date/Datum/Fecha/Date:

- A supply of stationery for follow-up letters.
- A supply of passport photographs for forms.
- Several good copies of your CV for further use.
- Copies of your letter of application/application form to refresh your own memory of what you said.
- Samples of your work, where relevant and practical. For example, your sketches/designs if a designer.
- References or letters of recommendation, and some copies.
- Certificates for academic and professional qualifications. Most employers will accept photocopies but, in Europe, copies should be signed/stamped by the issuing authority to confirm their authenticity.
- Birth and marriage certificates. These may be needed in connection with work and residence permits.

How should you handle the interview?

Interview styles vary across Europe. In some places, especially Germany, Switzerland, Austria and Scandinavia, you might encounter a very formal interview. Elsewhere, even in France, it may consist of an interview at a café table under a shady tree! Generally, however, all countries are more formal than the UK where more casual American-style methods are often the case.

What types of interview are there?

There are three main types of interview. Try to find out which one will apply and prepare accordingly. Often, the secretary/receptionist will tell you if you ring in advance and ask them. The types are:

- informal chat
- one-to-one interview
- panel interview.

A good procedure is to treat the informal chat like a formal interview, but be a little more relaxed: it could be an attempt to catch you off guard.

In panel interviews pay most attention to the person who speaks most, but do acknowledge the other interviewer(s).

Arrival
Arrive five to ten minutes early, but in some places expect to be kept waiting a long time. Outside Germany and Scandinavia punctuality is seen as a vice rather than a virtue!

How to dress
It is safest to assume that dress is formal for interviews, except in warm climates. In every European country, style, quality and fashion are taken more seriously than in the UK. Invariably, expensive, well made clothes *do* impress when applying for business and professional posts. In both France and Germany the British have a reputation for not being well dressed!

What language should you use?
Generally, if the job was advertised in the English language you can expect the interview to be conducted in English. If it was advertised in the local language you should expect to handle it in that language. Overall it is best not to suggest your command of the local language is better than it is. If you are not required to speak the local language then a few words of it, as a greeting or whatever, will probably impress. France is virtually the only country where a poor command of the local language will *not* be forgiven.

If you have a fair command of the local language, but are not necessarily fluent, it is often a good idea to make it clear you are unwilling to be interviewed in that language. Any well-organised interviewer who wishes to test your command of the local language should be prepared to arrange a separate test.

What should you say at interview?

An interview for any job should be very similar in content in any country. There are, though, slight differences when you are setting out to work abroad. It is rarely appropriate to allow the interview to run in the same way as one for a national of that country. Whilst there are surely disadvantages in being an expatriate there are also many advantages, and these must be exploited. You should consider raising the following points:

- The advantages that your knowledge of your trade/profession in the UK will bring to the employer.

- The advantages that your knowledge of working/business practices in the UK will bring to the employer.
- Your knowledge of the employer's country (research beforehand).
- Your knowledge of the employer's business (research beforehand).
- How well you feel able to adapt to working changes (and how well you are aware of them).
- Your view of 'Europe' as a whole. How will things be in future?

Of course, you should be prepared for the interviewer to raise his/her own points. The interviewer might ask some awkward questions with regard to working in a foreign country, and you may want to be prepared to answer them. They could include:

- Why do you want to leave your present employer?
- Why do you want to move out of the UK?
- Why do you want this job?
- Why do you want to live in . . . Austria?
- What problems do you envisage and how will you adapt at work?
- How will your family adapt?
- Where do you want to be in five years and where do you feel this company will be?

Experience suggests that individual interviewers are not necessarily committed Europeans or committed to the employment of expatriates, even if their employer or their company's employment policy is. Hence, more resolute answers may be needed than would be the case for a job in the UK.

Post interview procedure

It is usually a good idea to write a short note of thanks after the interview. However, do check, as in some places it is unacceptable to appear to be canvassing the interviewer. Conversely, in other places, such as

Italy, it is considered essential to follow up contacts and, indeed, only candidates who do so are likely to be seriously considered. Again, the interviewer's receptionist or secretary may be prepared to advise you.

The follow-up note is a good opportunity to pass on contact addresses — both back in the UK if returning home directly, plus an address abroad, even if a hotel one.

Even if you are unsuccessful at interview it can be a good idea to keep in touch with the company in question and periodically reintroduce yourself. In most European countries, especially Spain, Portugal, Greece and Italy, contacts are so important and an employer who does not or cannot recruit you may recommend you to colleagues, or pass on other useful information.

SECURING A POSTING INTO EUROPE

In the past a posting was the most usual way of finding a job in Europe. Now, although this is set to continue, it is by no means the main way. Companies will undoubtedly move their staff across Europe, but international posting is rarely used to fill more than three per cent of vacancies, even in the most enthusiastic companies. Indeed, in recent years the total number of people going abroad has increased but the number of postings has slightly declined.

In most cases a job secured by posting will be for a **fixed term contract** (typically one, three or five years) rather than indefinitely. Salaries are also sometimes higher and further benefits are offered beyond the normal scope of the job: for example, relocation benefits, housing allowances and school fees. Generally, though, these benefits do not compensate for the fact that relying on a posting alone will stand you a much lower chance of finding a job in Europe than direct application.

The following pointers will be of use in locating posting opportunities and identifying yourself as a candidate:

- Transfer your job to a company with stronger European ties. Chamber of Commerce membership lists are a pointer here.
- Ask your current employer if they have any European branches, subsidiaries, etc. Sometimes these are not widely known; refer to the directory *Who Owns Whom* for guidance.
- Ask your professional association or trade union about any overseas links.

- Check staff bulletins and newsletters for opportunities and clues.
- Contact your immediate boss or personnel officer and ask to be considered for any posts that come up. It is often generally assumed that people don't want to be posted, so those who express an interest are often remembered when the time comes.
- Ask if you can write to any European subsidiaries or branches to see if they have vacancies.
- Ask for introductions to any European subsidiaries or branches. Visit them if possible to discuss possibilities.
- Ask if you can canvass any suppliers or customers in Europe for possible vacancies (not strictly a posting but often quite practical).

Even if you decide to aim for a posting then do remember to keep looking for a job by direct application. If your company is not already an active poster it may take years for a vacancy to arise.

4

What is Working in Europe Like?

HOW THE SINGLE EUROPEAN MARKET AFFECTS WORKING IN THE EU

The Single European Market, which came into being in 1993, has some implications for the European job seeker but these are generally not as widespread as might be expected.

Although **tariffs** and **quotas** had not applied between EU countries for many years, it became apparent in the 1970s that several non-tariff barriers were still hampering inter-European trade. A commitment to remove these non-tariff barriers was officially made by the signing of the **Single European Act** (SEA) in 1986 and this became effective on 1 January 1993.

The SEA had several aims. One was to eliminate frontier controls. Another was to harmonise product standards all over Europe. Both these aims and others are designed to permit better inter-European trade. The only commitments which directly affect those working are to remove frontier controls — no **work permits** are now needed to work in the EU — and to mutually recognise professional qualifications. Other commitments, such as harmonising product standards, make it easier to work in another country but are not intended to encourage working elsewhere in the community as such.

There is no EU commitment to encourage EU citizens to work in other EU countries. It is simply easier to work in an EU country than it was, but that is a means to an end (fuller competition) not an end in its own right.

Although there are EU regulations covering employment law, working hours and holiday entitlements, when working in a particular country it is the employment laws of that country which apply, not EU regulations as such. The laws in some countries coincide, but in others they do not. In all situations where EU directives are in force (such as recognition of qualifications) it is the EU regulations which take precedence over national laws.

WHAT ARE YOUR RIGHTS IN THE EU?

Citizens of EU countries have the right to live and to work in any of the other EU countries. Having a job used to be a precondition of this, but now this is not necessarily the case. EU countries cannot apply a visa or work permit requirement on other EU citizens.

However, entry to a country is not automatic. Health, financial and public security reasons can be used to deny entry, though they rarely are.

Citizens of EU countries are entitled to be considered for jobs on the same basis as locals. The only jobs they may be prevented from taking are those connected with state security, such as the police force. EU citizens can apply for most jobs with EU governments and with nationalised industries.

None of these basic rights removes the need to be qualified for the work in question. You will also be expected to be competent in the local language. There is, therefore, no reason why a Briton should not work for Deutsche Bundesbahn (German state railways), but you would need to be at least as suitable as a local applicant.

WORKING OUTSIDE THE EU

So far the situation in the EU has brought about a few changes to working in non-EU European countries. The advent of the European Economic Area (EEA) should grant employment rights to EU citizens in other EEA member states (Norway, Iceland, Liechtenstein and Switzerland) but the situation varies. Norway is now open to EU citizens seeking work but Switzerland still positively discourages them.

It is still more difficult to get work in the EEA countries than the EU countries. The best way to regard the situation is that non-nationals of those countries are usually only employed where there are no suitable nationals willing and able to do the job. This means that most of the jobs offered to foreigners are for the qualified or experienced.

The eastern European countries are a little more liberal and tentatively welcome foreigners who are contributing to their development.

WORK PERMITS

Do I need a work permit?

Work permits are required whenever a non-national seeks a job in a foreign country. The major exclusion is that EU citizens *do not need* any sort of work permit or other consent to work in *another EU country*.

Work permits are usually only granted to those who have found a job. It is generally necessary to be outside the country when applying. Some professions in some countries are forbidden to non-nationals and a permit will not be granted.

How and where to obtain a work permit

The following procedure is advisable if you are looking to work *outside* the EU:

1. Contact the London embassy/consulate of the country you are interested in. Get details of permit requirements.

2. Find a suitable job. You can travel to most countries to find a job but cannot enter to work without a permit.

3. If offered a job accept it 'subject to permit'. Ask the employer for a contract of employment.

4. Apply for a work permit, usually from the London embassy or consulate. This procedure can take from four weeks to six months depending on the country. In some countries it is the employer, not you, who must apply for the permit.

5. Confirm your job with the employer and travel out to take it up.

Work permits may last for a fixed period or the duration of the job.

RESIDENCE PERMITS

Non-EU countries

Foreigners going to live and work in non-EU countries always require residence permits. These are usually granted subject to having a job and a work permit. Check with the respective embassy as to whether the permit should be applied for *before* entering the country or once you have arrived. Residence permits are usually valid for a fixed period only and renewable; one year or five years are most usual.

EU countries

Although EU citizens do not require work permits to work in another EU country, it is still necessary to have a residence permit to live there.

This can be applied for on arrival; it is not necessary to have the permit in advance.

EU citizens have a right of residence in other EU countries whether working, running a business, being a student, retired person or looking for work. If looking for work, the maximum stay permitted is three months. However, right of residence can be denied for reasons of public health or lack of finance, or even not having accommodation.

Although many countries — such as Germany — will readily grant residence permits to EU citizens, others such as France and Spain are more difficult. They are not entitled to withhold residence but they can make the procedure bureaucratically difficult in order to discourage new residents. It is often necessary to persist with your application.

Residence permits are combined with **identity cards** in some countries and are essential in order to make use of public services; this is particularly the case in Belgium. In the past residence permits were issued for a fixed period of one or five years. At the time of writing indefinite residence permits are being phased in.

How and where to apply for a residence permit

It is a good idea to start the application for a residence permit immediately after arrival, although most EU countries allow applications to be made within 90 days or so.

The embassy or consulate of the respective country will advise you of the procedure. However, permits are usually issued at the town hall of the town or city where you intend to reside. In some cases the main police station handles this instead. You will need the following documents:

- an application form
- your passport
- passport photographs (often up to six).

Requirements vary from country to country and office to office and some will also require such documents as:

- evidence of means (a bank statement from a local bank or cash; the amount varies from country to country)
- deeds showing property purchased, or a lease
- birth and marriage certificates
- a health clearance certificate from a local hospital (in some places).

As a result it pays to be prepared before leaving the UK. Even within the EU there are no uniform requirements, and although you may be entitled to a residence permit each country can apply its own procedure.

Dependants of those granted work and residence permits are usually granted automatic residence if the head of family is granted residence, but must still apply for a permit.

CONTRACTS OF EMPLOYMENT

Do I need a contract of employment?

National laws in all European countries state that you have a legal requirement to a contract of employment but, as in the UK, whether this is easy to obtain from an employer is a different matter. However, if working in a non-EU country you must request one in advance to present to the embassy or consulate in order to obtain a work permit and residence permit. Some EU countries may require that EU citizens have a contract in order to obtain a residence permit, but application of this is patchy.

European employers are of both the reputable and less reputable kind as in the UK, so a contract of employment will always be a good idea. Some employers may be reluctant to issue them, and if this is the case check to see if they are not intending you to work on a cash-in-hand, no-tax-deducted basis. This is endemic in parts of Spain, Greece and particularly Italy.

What should a contract of employment include?

There is no standard contract of employment, even within the EU, and contracts are drawn up and followed according to law and custom in each respective country. Take legal advice on this locally if necessary. Only those working for UK companies in Europe are likely to receive a contract in English and governed by English law.

A contract of employment may be a long, notarised document, or a simple letter of agreement, but its basic provisions should include at least the following:

- job description
- details of duties
- responsible to?
- hours of work
- salary: day rate or piece rate or salaried
- length of contract
- notice required to leave

- grounds for dismissal
- grievance procedure.

In many cases terms and conditions of service are negotiable, but only within the legal framework of each individual country.

HOW DO WAGES AND SALARIES COMPARE?

Rates of pay in Europe

As a general rule, workers in most western European countries receive a higher gross pay than their counterparts in the UK for any given type of work. This is tempered by different rates of taxation and different living costs, but the gross figure expected should always be much higher. In addition, in mainland Europe, the highest salary earners tend to earn comparatively much more than the lower paid.

Country	Average Pay	Average cost of living
France	30%-50% more than UK	5% less than UK
Germany	50%-75% more	10%-15% more
Spain	20% less to 20% more	5% less
Belgium	30%-45% more	up to 5% more
Netherlands	30%-40% more	up to 5% more
Portugal	30%-50% less	20% less
Italy	up to 50% more	20%-25% more
Greece	20%-50% less	20%-40% less
Austria	50%-100% more	10%-25% more
Switzerland	100%-200% more	30%-50% more
Scandinavia	15%-50% more	60%-100% more

Fig. 10. Comparative pay in European countries.

Eastern Europe rates of pay vary from executive level to voluntary work status. Currently, rates of pay in the former eastern Germany have still not achieved full parity with western Germany.

Some countries have a legal minimum rate of pay, such as the SMIC in France.

Fringe benefits

Fewer fringe benefits are on offer in most European countries than in the UK and the bottom line salary figure is much more representative of the actual package, except in France where benefits are often considered more important than actual salary. European employers, unlike those in some parts of the world, do not actually offer large relocation packages, fares out, accommodation and school fees. There is usually no need for them to do so unless courting a particularly sought-after employee.

The benefits that do exist are often very different to the UK. You might ask for the following:

- Company cars. These are much rarer in most countries but it is cheaper to buy and run a car in many anyway.

- Productivity bonus. This is becoming popular in some countries.

- Thirteenth-month bonus (double pay in one month of the year). In many cases, however, this should not be seen as a bonus but merely a different way of splitting the salary.

- Health/social security contributions. Few countries have a free national health service. Contributions are paid by employers in most countries either by law or voluntarily. You may be offered extra health benefits as an incentive.

- Accommodation allowances. Popular in a few countries, such as Germany.

Pay bargaining procedures

All the European countries, with the exception of Eastern Europe and Greece, have highly organised systems for pay bargaining and you should check this out if interested. In many countries, such as France, bargaining is done between employees' bodies or trades unions and employers at regional level, rather than nationally, and the subsequent pay rise applies to all workers in the same industry, whether or not in the trade union etc. Such changes would also apply to an expatriate worker. There are no EU-wide regulations on minimum pay and pay bargaining as yet.

Hotel manager, Spain	£28,500
Shop assistant, Marseille	£18,230
English teacher, Lisbon	£7,200
Water engineer, Greece	£18,900
Warehouse manager, Moscow	US$60,000
Aircraft technician, Amsterdam	£22,340
Secretary, Calais	£17,580

(Figures compiled from jobs advertised at time of writing.)

Fig. 11. Some examples of European pay.

WHAT WORKING CONDITIONS CAN I EXPECT?

Working hours

Regardless of European regulations working hours are already fairly similar all across Europe, and broadly similar to those in the UK at around 38-40 hours per week. Scandinavians typically work 40 hours, though some other countries are trying to reduce to 37 hours. The working week is Monday to Friday; Saturday morning working in France and Belgium is rarely the norm now. Most European countries take a long lunch hour which is regarded as sacrosanct. The siesta is still popular in the hotter countries, but has often been shortened in modern offices. All the European countries tend to start and finish work a little earlier (starting at 7.30am-8.30am) than the UK.

In many countries overtime can only be undertaken after permission from a local labour inspector and must be paid at 150-200 per cent of the standard rate.

Holiday entitlement

Paid holiday entitlement in most countries is higher than in the UK. In most the minimum entitlement is four weeks; but in all countries employees expect more as a recruitment incentive. Holiday entitlements tend to be higher in central and northern Europe and lower in the south and east. Southern Europeans may not take a summer holiday as such but elsewhere a three week summer break is expected. In some places, such as France, it is still common for a company to close completely for a full month in summer.

Women working in Europe

All the information in this book relates equally to men and women, but most of the countries of Europe exhibit some disparity when it comes to employing women. Some countries are more forward looking than the UK, others are backward.

Most countries encourage women to work, and most give them equal rights by law, though EU-wide equal rights legislation is not yet operative. However, it is the situation in practice that matters. In some countries women do mostly menial work. In other countries they are restricted to the traditionally female types of work like teaching and nursing. In others there are few women executives. In some, however, women executives seem to get much further than in the UK.

Most countries pledge equal wages for equal work but in practice different rates may apply to men and women.

Working conditions and trade unions

Most European countries have good working conditions, and laws for the protection of the workforce are advanced. The Scandinavian countries are very advanced in this respect. Within the EU, Greece and Spain tend to be less enthusiastic about labour legislation than many other countries.

Trades unions operate in all countries, but their power and influence vary considerably and in most cases have declined in recent years. In France, once a militant trade union country, they are only active in the older industries. In many countries works councils and employees' bodies are more popular. Where such organisations do exist non-nationals are entitled to join. Membership is rarely compulsory but there may be situations where it is advisable. Check locally.

Labour rights and working conditions will eventually be standardised EU-wide; at the moment the UK is less enthusiastic about this than other countries.

DEALING WITH PROBLEMS AT WORK

Avoiding problems

At the moment most governments of EU countries tentatively support the idea of free movement of labour. Usually, however, they are more concerned about promoting these rights for their nationals rather than reciprocally. In the workplace, however, employers and employees tend to be flattered that a foreigner should want to work in their country. The Germans, for example, tend to like British workers. The French have been traditionally most hostile to foreign workers, but hostility is much rarer nowadays. Rivalry, however, may be intense.

COUNTRY	SITUATION
France	Similar to UK. Many women in top jobs in Paris. Fewer in the south.
Germany	Women find it harder to attain top positions. Germany is the only country to have little legislation against sex discrimination.
Belgium	Similar to UK.
Netherlands	Prospects generally better than UK.
Denmark	Has a well implemented equal rights policy.
Spain	Women mostly in menial work. Women may find it very hard to attain executive status.
Portugal	Women not expected to do more than menial work but equal rights legislation is some of the most comprehensive in Europe.
Italy	Women preferred in traditional roles but there are many successful working women.
Greece	Women preferred to stay at home.
Switzerland	Slightly better prospects than UK.
Austria	Slightly better prospects than UK.
Norway	Women have well defined rights but few aim for top positions.
Sweden	Has a well implemented equal rights policy.
E. Europe	Women can do most jobs but few are qualified for more senior jobs, except medicine.

Fig. 12. How working women fare in European countries.

You will want to make an effort to fit in, but it is often not a good idea to be too 'local'. This can be resented in some countries, especially the Latin ones. Often the best way to be accepted by colleagues or subordinates is to ask for their help in settling in — rather than being seen to be a 'new brush sweeping clean' — even if you have been recruited for your experience or qualifications.

If possible, try to think ahead to avoid problems, which often include:

- language barriers greater than expected
- resistance of nationals to outside involvement
- misunderstandings/differences in standards
- lack of foreign sensitivity towards local customs
- more formality in business in most countries than the UK
- lack of, or excess of, technology.

And, just as importantly:

- overestimating/underestimating the challenge
- disruption to daily life
- spouse/children unable to settle.

How to solve problems

Some countries have advanced procedures for care of their employees, especially the Scandinavian countries. The central western European countries are progressing very quickly in this respect. In Spain, Greece, Portugal and some parts of Italy you may still find that formal arrangements for employee-care and solving problems have still to be devised.

A general tip is that it is always worth raising problems at work as soon as they occur. Quite often, employers and employees will not have anticipated these problems themselves but may be more flexible than might be expected. The following sources of assistance should be sought, and in this order:

- Your immediate superior: hierarchy of staff is important in most countries and care must be taken not to inadvertently bypass a superior.

- Company management, personnel management or director.

- Works council or trade union: in some countries (such as Germany) disputes must usually be referred to the court by a works council.

- The courts: the law can be called upon to deal with severe problems and disputes, *eg* unfair dismissal or redundancy. This should always be considered a last resort. In some countries, such as Greece and

Spain, it is practically impossible for foreigners to bring labour cases before the courts except at great cost. Even in the more organised countries, like Germany, it can take two or three years for a case to be heard. The emphasis should always be on finding an employer and job which offer minimum possibility for dispute in the first place.

5

Employment Guide

AUSTRIA

What is the overall potential?

As a small country Austria does not have an enormous number of job vacancies; what expatriate jobs there are, are more readily taken by the Swiss or Germans. Nevertheless Austria is an advanced country, more industrialised than is often realised, and so some opportunities may be available.

Main industries

- light manufacturing/engineering
- iron and steel
- textiles and clothing
- food products
- chemicals and paper products.

Agriculture is still important, as is tourism, predominantly in winter.

Employment for foreigners

Expatriates are attracted to Austria for most types of work but are principally, as in many other countries, either executive/professional in senior positions or casual working travellers. Expatriates tend to be employed in small but significant numbers in the engineering and textile industries, computing and finance. Qualified teachers are sometimes needed. Casual workers work mainly in tourism, hotels and catering. Au pairs are also accepted.

Advice to job-hunters

Opportunities for British people who do not speak good Austrian

German are very limited. It is, therefore, unwise to travel to Austria without a job already arranged, although some working travellers do this.

Finding sources of work

No UK agencies deal with Austria on a regular basis and there are no Austrian agencies offering permanent work.

The state employment service

The Austrian state employment offices are known as the **Landesarbeitsamt**.

The Landesarbeitsamt can only help personal callers who speak good German. If enquiring about Austrian vacancies from the UK then use the EURES system.

Using newspapers

Austrian newspapers offer some vacancies for expatriates and can be used for advertising. The main ones are *Die Press*, *Der Standard*, and *Wiener Zeitung* (Vienna), *Neue Tiroler Zeitung*, and *Tiroler Tageszeitung* (Innsbruck) and *Neues Salzburger Tagblatt*, *Salzburger Nachrichten* and *Salzburger Volkszeitung* (Salzburg). The Munich (Germany) newspapers sometimes also advertise vacancies in Austria.

Making direct applications

Speculative applications can be made direct to employers. A list of companies with possible executive vacancies is available to purchase from:

The Austrian Chamber of Commerce, Turkenstrasse 9
A-1090 Vienna.
Tel: 0043 1515200

Working travellers should approach hotels, bars and restaurants, which will often offer casual work, official or unofficial.

Work for young people

Young people seeking holiday work can obtain information/tips from:

The Austrian Committee for the International Exchange of Students (OKISTA)
Turkenstrasse 6–8, A-1090 Vienna.
Tel: 0043 1 401 480
Fax: 0043 1 401 48 7100
Web: http://www.oekista.co.at

What are working conditions like?

Working conditions in Austria

Average salary	Executive	£42,800
	Skilled worker	£26,500
Working week	38 hours	
Holiday entitlement	28 days	
Minimum fringe benefits	Productivity bonuses are becoming popular.	
Income tax rate	16-33 per cent	
Unemployment rate	4 per cent	
Trade unions	Works organisations are popular.	

Living conditions

Living conditions in Austria

Living costs	Higher than UK but not quite as high as Switzerland	
Average 3-bed house	To buy	£110,000
	To rent (month)	£ 1,500
Social security system	Deductions are made from wages to provide a wide range of state benefits. A reciprocal agreement on social security exists between the UK and Austria and free or reduced cost hospital treatment is available.	
Education	Good. There are several International Schools.	
Standard of living	High.	

Entry regulations

EU citizens do not require work or residence permits. However, those wishing to reside in Austria must have either employment or adequate financial resources to support themselves. An ID card (Lichtbildausweis für Fremde) must be obtained within three months of arrival. This is available at labour offices or main police stations.

Embassies

Austrian Embassy
18 Belgrave Mews West
London SW1X 8HU.
Tel: (020) 7235 3731
Fax: (020) 7344 0292
Email: embassy@austria.org.uk

British Embassy
Jauresgasse 12
A-1030 Vienna.
Tel: 01 716 130

Major UK companies in Austria

Beecham, Castrol, Cadbury Schweppes, Croda, EMI, Glaxo, Hoover, ICI, ICL, Lever Brothers, Rank Xerox, Shell, Standard Chartered Bank, Thorn EMI.

Language courses

Berlitz, 9–13 Grosvenor Street, London W1A 3BZ. Tel: (020) 7915 0909. In Vienna: Tel: (0222) 512 8286.

Internationale Sprachschulen-Foundation, 8010 Graz, Kreuzg 46/1. Tel: 0316 386166.

Further information is available from the Anglo-Austrian Society, 46 Queen Anne's Gate, London SW1H 9AU. Tel: (020) 7222 0366.

Other useful contacts

Austriahotels, Archgate Centre, 823A High Road, London N12. Tel: (020) 8446 1306.

Austrian Airlines, 10 Wardour Street, London W1. Tel: (020) 7434 7350.

Austrian National Tourist Office, 30 St George's Street, London W1. Tel: (020) 7269 0461.

Austrian Trade Commission, 45 Princes Gate, London SW7 2QA. Tel: (020) 7584 4411 Fax: (020) 7584 2565.

Austrian Cultural Institute, 28 Rutland Gate, London SW7. Tel: (020) 7584 8653.
British Council, Schenkenstrasse 4, A-1010 Vienna. Tel: 533 2616/8.

BELGIUM

What is the overall potential?

Belgium has never been a popular country for UK workers, despite being one of our nearest neighbours with excellent transport links. Population is small at ten million and the country is overshadowed commercially by France and Germany. Unemployment is a perennial problem. That said, Belgium is at the very centre of the European Community and indeed many expatriate jobs are with the EU institutions in Brussels.

To all intents and purposes Belgium should be thought of as two separate states — Wallonia in the south where French is spoken, and Flanders in the north where Flemish (similar to Dutch) is spoken. Brussels is a separate region which is officially bilingual and in many respects multilingual.

Main industries

Some of Belgium's main industries are old and traditional and in decline. These include:

- coal
- steel
- textiles
- heavy engineering.

New industries include:

- petrochemicals
- aerospace
- computing
- pharmaceuticals
- electronics.

Motor manufacture is popular, and transport and communications sectors are expanding fast.

Employment for foreigners

Executive, professional and skilled

A large number of foreigners working in Belgium are there in an executive/professional capacity, for which there are very few opportunities outside Brussels. However, opportunities are becoming available for junior management and clerical staff, and some skilled tradesmen have found opportunities. For work with the EU see later in this chapter.

Casual

Belgium is one of the few countries where foreigners can do all types of casual work: try hotel, catering, cleaning and shop work. There is a small tourist industry. Unemployment means that, though these jobs are plentiful, competition for them is heavy. Special laws prevent temporary work in the construction industry.

Advice to job-hunters

Compared with other states Belgium is a small country and your search for employment should largely be confined to Brussels, where the vast majority of the available jobs are. Some knowledge of French is essential for most jobs; a knowledge of Flemish (similar to Dutch) will increase the number of vacancies available to you.

Finding sources of work

Recruitment links between the UK and Belgium are not strong; in many cases it is easier to get a job on the spot. Qualified personnel stand a reasonable chance by applying to the Overseas Placing Unit (OPU).

Otherwise try private UK agencies, though few deal with Belgium on a large scale. Private employment agencies exist in Belgium and are numerous in Brussels, especially for temporary jobs, but rarer elsewhere. Locate through Belgian *Yellow Pages* at main UK libraries. One of the main multilingual office staff agencies is:

Avenue Louise Interim
207 avenue Louise
1050 Brussels.
Tel: (02) 640 91 91

ECCO is at:

27a Rue de l'Abbaye
1050 Brussels.
Tel: (02) 647 87 80
Fax: (02) 640 66 97

The state employment service

The state employment agency in Flanders is called VDAB, in Wallonia it is called FOREM and in Brussels ORBEM. Each agency deals in jobs in the respective regional language. A list of all offices is available from head office at:

blvd Anspach 65
1000 Brussels.
Tel: 505 14 11
Fax: 511 30 52
Web: http://www.orbem.be

Main office for visits is at: 38 rue d'Escalier, 1000 Brussels.

Temporary or casual work can be obtained through the T-service bureaux in most cities. In Brussels this is at 69 Boulevard Anspach.

Using newspapers

Newspapers are a good source of vacancies. The main ones are *Le Soir* (Brussels), especially the Tuesday edition, *Antwerpse Morgen* (Antwerp) and *La Meusse* (Liege). Also see Brussels' freesheet papers *Belgique No 1* and *L'Echo*. Working travellers will find jobs through or can place advertisements in an excellent English language newspaper called *The Bulletin* at:

1038 Chaussée de Waterloo
B-1180 Brussels.
Tel: (02) 373 99 09
Fax: (02) 375 98 22

Making direct applications

Speculative applications can be made direct to employers. Addresses from *Yellow Pages* (*Pages Jaunes* or *Gouden Gids* depending on the language of the particular area), which are at some UK libraries, and on the internet in English at www.teldir.com/eng.

What are working conditions like?

Belgians are a little more relaxed in their work than the French or Germans. However, good language ability is taken for granted and Belgians are very committed to the idea of being good Europeans. Employment legislation is very comprehensive and tends to favour the employee.

Working conditions in Belgium

Average salary	Executive	£35,000
	Skilled worker	£20,350
Working week	40 hours	
Holiday entitlement	Four weeks and ten public holidays	
Minimum fringe benefits	13th month and productivity bonuses	
Income tax rate	25-72 per cent	
Trade unions	Very active but membership voluntary	

Living conditions

Belgium is often a country criticised as lacking any character, but this is largely unfair. If anything, it is highly successful as a multilingual country and in a better position to take advantage of the European Union than any other country. Brussels is a very cosmopolitan city, with a large British population, but other places can be remarkably provincial.

Living conditions in Belgium

Living costs	Slightly more than UK. Food more, but cars much cheaper.	
Average 3-bed house	To buy	£100,000
	To rent (month)	£950
Social security system	Comprehensive. All employees must contribute 10 per cent of their wages to an insurance fund (Mutualité or Ziekenfond) which pays 70-80 per cent of medical bills.	
Education	Free to EU nationals. English schools available in Brussels.	
Standard of living	Very high. Belgium combines the best of several European countries.	

Residence permits

EU nationals do not need work permits but must have a residence permit. Apply within three months of arrival, at the local town hall. For stays of a further six months you will be given a **Temporary Residence Card**, after that you will be issued with a Belgian Identity Card.

Embassies

Belgian Embassy
103 Eaton Square.
London SW1W 9AB
Tel: (020) 7470 3700
Email: info@belgium.embassy.co.uk
Web: http://www.belgium.embassy.co.uk

British Embassy
Rue d'Arlon 85
1040 Brussels.

Tel: (02) 287 62 11
Fax: (02) 287 63 60
Web: http://www.british-embassy.be

Major UK companies in Belgium

BAT, BP, Barclays Bank, British Steel, Cadbury Schweppes, EMI, Fisons, ICI, ICL, Lever Brothers, Marks & Spencer, Proctor & Gamble, Shell, Smith & Nephew.

Language courses

French

Berlitz: 9–13 Grosvenor Street, London W1A 3BZ. Tel: (020) 7915 0909. In Brussels: Tel: (02) 649 6175.
Alliance Française, Rue d'Arlon 24, 1050 Ixelles. Tel: (02) 502 33 77.

French/Flemish

Inlingua, 28 Rotton Park Road, Birmingham B16 9JL. Tel: (0121) 454 0204.
CPAB, 29-31 Chaussée d'Ixelles, Brussels. Tel: (02) 511 0109.

Also see listings under France and Netherlands.

More useful contacts

Anglo-Belgian Club, 60 Knightsbridge, London SW1X 7LF.Tel: (020) 7235 5642.
Belgo-Luxembourg Chamber of Commerce, Berkeley House, 73 Upper Richmond Road, London SW15 2SZ. Tel: (020) 8877 9268.
Lingua Leeds, 8 Kingswood Gardens, Leeds LS8 2BT. Tel: (0113) 266 5378.

Government offices, etc.

Administration des Douanes et Accises (Belgian Customs Office), boulevard d'Ypres 41, 1000-Brussels. Tel: (02) 225 14 41.
British Consulate, Korte Klarenstraat 7, 2000-Antwerp. Tel: (03) 232 6940 Fax: (03) 231 1200.
European Commission, rue de la Loi 200, 1049-Brussels. Tel: +32 2 299 Web: www.europa.eu.int
Institut National de Statistiques, Place Albert 1er 4, 6000-Charleroi. Tel: (071) 304301.
Ministère des Affaires Economiques (Belgian Ministry of Economic

Affairs), Square du Meeus 26, 1040-Brussels. Tel: (02) 506 51 11 Fax: (02) 514 24 72.

Ministère des Affairs Etrangères (Belgian Ministry of Foreign Affairs), 15 Rue des Petits Carmes, Karmelietenstraat 15, B-1000 Brussels. Tel: (32) 2 501 81 11 Fax: (32) 2 501 84 96.

Ministry of Education (Dutch speaking), Rijksadminstratief Centrum, Arcadengebouw, Blok F, 1010-Brussels. Tel: (02) 210 5111.

Ministry of Education (French speaking), Cité Administrative de l'État, boulevard Pachéco, 1010-Brussels. Tel: (02) 210 5620.

Office du Commerce Extérieur (Belgian Foreign Trade Office), boulevard du Roi Albert II 30, 1000-Brussels. Tel: (02) 206 35 11 Fax: (02) 203 18 12.

Office Nationale de l'Emploi, boulevard de l'Empereur 7, 1000-Brussels. Tel: (02) 515 41 11.

Travel

Belgian National Tourist Office, rue Marché aux Herbes 61, 1000-Brussels. Tel: (02) 504 03 90 Fax: (02) 5044 02 70 Web: http://www.belgium-tourism.net; or Olmenlaan 11, 610-Antwerp. Tel: (03) 830 54 48.

Belgium Tourist Reservations (BTR), bvd Anspach, 1000-Brussels. Tel: (02) 513 74 84.

Belgian National Railways,156 Blackfriars Road, London SE1 8EN. Tel: (020) 7593 2332.

Belgian National Tourist Office, 29 Princes Street, London W1R 7RG. Tel: 0891 887799. Premier House, 2 Gayton Road, Harrow, Middlesex HA1 2XU. Tel: (020) 8861 3300.

Belgian World Airlines, Sabena, Flight Enquiries, Heathrow Airport, Hounslow. Tel: (020) 8759 1033.

British Airways, Centre International Rogier, bte 144, 9th floor, 1210-Brussels. Tel: (02) 548 2133.

Hoverspeed, Natienkaai 5, 8400-Ostende. Tel: (059) 55 99 17.

Immatriculation des Vehicles, Ministère du Transport, rue de la Loi 65, 1040-Brussels. Tel: (02) 237 6711 Fax: (02) 230 1824 Web: http://www.belgium.fgov.be

Royal Automobile Club de Belgique, rue d'Arlon 53, 1000-Brussels. Tel: (02) 287 0911.

Sabena, Avenue Mouniere 2, 1200 Brussels. Tel: (02) 770 5697.

Touring Club de Belgique, rue de la Loi 44, 1000-Brussels. Tel: (02) 233 2211.

British Banks

HSBC Bank Plc, Louizalaan 326/15. 1050-Elsene, Brussels. Tel: (02) 639 2770 Fax (02) 639 2789.

Lloyds Bank (Belgium), Tervurenlaan 2, 1040-Etterbeek, Brussels. Tel: (02) 739 59 34 Fax (02) 733 1107.

Newspapers (for job adverts, accommodation, etc.)

Le Soir, place de Louvain 21, 1000-Brussels.

De Standaard, Vlaamse Uitgevers Maatsschappij, A Gossetlaan 30A, 1720-Groot-Bijgaarden.

Other organisations

British Chamber of Commerce for Belgium and Luxembourg, Britannia House, rue Joseph II 30, 1040-Brussels. Tel: (02) 540 9030.

British Council, 15 rue de la Charite, 1210-Brussels. Tel: (02) 227 0840 (English lending library, lectures and conferences).

INBEL, Boulevard du Regent 54, 1000-Brussels Tel: (02) 512 51 25 (information pamphlets and booklets on Belgian art, sport, history, the monarchy, statistics, universities, etc.)

Business and economy

Insight Guide: Belgium (Insight Publications; annual publication; includes articles on company formation, finance and taxation, legal considerations, manufacturing in Belgium, exporting to Belgium, Belgium as an economic and communications centre and services available.)

Cooking

Hamelcourt, Juliette Elkon, *A Belgian Cookbook* (1996).

Travel

Blyth, Derek, *Flemish Cities Explored: Bruges, Ghent, Antwerp, Mechelen and Brussels* (Pallas Athene 1999).

Belgium (APA Publications 1999) 95pp.

Dunford, Martin and Lee, Phil, *Belgium and Luxembourg: the Rough Guide* (Rough Guides 1999)

Everyman Guide to Brussels (Everyman Travel Guides 1996) 360pp.

Fodor's Belgium and Luxembourg (Fodor's Travel Guides 1991).

Hart, John, *German and Belgian Rock Climbs: an Interim Guide Book* (Cordee 1988).

Hazlewood, Carole, *Long Stays in Belgium and Luxembourg* (Hippocrene Books US 1987).

Logan, Leanne and Cole, Geert, *Brussels, Bruges & Antwerp* (Lonely Planet Publications 1999) 248pp.

Government publications

Country Profile: Belgium (Department of Trade and Industry 1990).

Hints to Exporters Visiting Belgium and Luxembourg (pocket-sized guide; Department of Trade and Industry 1989/90; available from DTI Publications, Orderline Admail 528, London SW1W 8YT. Tel: 0870 1502 500 Fax: 0870 1502 333 Email: dtipubs@ echristian.co.uk

Marketing Consumer Goods in Belgium (Department of Trade and Industry 1986).

Unemployment Benefit in the Community (UBL22, available from Unemployment Benefit Offices).

Working Abroad (Leaflet available from Job Centres).

European Community publications

Social Security for Migrant Workers: Belgium (Office for Official Publications of the European Communities 1985).

The European Community publishes many reports, surveys and other studies. To obtain a full list of materials, write to the European Commission, rue de la Loi 22, B-1049 Brussels; or the Office for Official Publications of the European Communities, Unit OP/3 Publications, 2 rue Mercier, L-2985 Luxembourg. Email: idea@opoce.cec.be

---

DENMARK

What is the overall potential?

Denmark is one of the smaller European countries and is better known for its agriculture rather than its industrial production. Because of this it is by no means easy to find a job in Denmark, but this country is one of the most open and forward looking in Europe. It has implemented more EU directives than any other, by far.

Main industries

Denmark is largely an agricultural and manufacturing country but most industries are very modern and efficient; it is not a simple, agricultural economy. Meat, dairy and processed food products have an enormous market in countries such as the UK. Other industries include:

- light engineering
- electrical engineering
- textiles
- paper production
- fisheries
- brewing.

Oil and gas exploration and exploitation are growing in importance.

Employment for foreigners (all types)

It is difficult to identify types of jobs taken by foreigners in Denmark as they are well distributed through most types of industry. It is not particularly easy to find a position at any level, as there is plenty of local competition. Executive/professional staff would need to be highly competent. Medical staff are sometimes in short supply and the oil industry recruits British personnel, as does the large Danish shipping industry. For casual workers, there is a small tourist industry based on Copenhagen, together with work in catering, cleaning, hotels and work on farms, fruit picking, etc to be had in summer and autumn.

Advice to job-hunters

Although English is widely spoken in Denmark, being able to speak some Danish is necessary for most jobs. Most expatriates will centre their search on Copenhagen alone.

Finding sources of work

Jobs can be found from UK or Denmark. Qualified personnel stand a good chance of being offered something suitable through OPU. Few private UK employment agencies have work to offer in Denmark. Private employment agencies will help foreigners (many speak English). In particular they can offer technical and scientific jobs, administrative or secretarial work and casual work. See the Danish *Yellow Pages*, available in a few UK libraries. Manpower is one of the main ones.

The state employment service

The state employment offices are the **Arbejdsformidlingen**. There are offices in all towns.

The chances of finding work here are good if you can speak or learn a little Danish.

Using newspapers

Newspapers to read or advertise in include *Politiken, Ekstra Bladet, Den*

Bla Auis, Belingske Tidende, especially on Sunday, and *Det Fri Aktuelt* (Copenhagen), *Fryens Stiftstidente* (Odense) and *Vestkysten* (Esbjerg). Executives should refer to the Danish trade and professional journals, details in *Benn's Media Directory International.*

Making direct applications
Speculative applications can be successful as most employers speak some English. Writing, telephoning or personal calling are all appropriate. See local *Yellow Pages* and *Kompass* directories for addresses. The Royal Danish Embassy can offer useful hints and *Facts about Denmark* booklet.

Work for young people
Young people seeking casual work could try the Studenternes Arbejdsformidlingen (Students Employment Agency). Information may also be available from Danmarks Internationale Studenterkomite.

What are working conditions like?

Denmark has extremely generous labour protection legislation.

Working conditions in Denmark

Average salary	Executive	£44,000
	Skilled worker	£28,000
Working week	37 hours	
Holiday entitlement	30 days and ten public holidays	
Minimum fringe benefits	State sickness, accident and unemployment provision is very generous; bonuses and paid training may be offered	
Income tax rate	28-87 per cent including social security	
Unemployment rate	7 per cent	
Trade unions	Very active. Most people are members of a union but labour relations are considered excellent.	

Conditions of service and pay are negotiated bi-annually and increased automatically at regular intervals. Denmark is a high-wage country but imposes some of the highest deductions in the world; the Danes take home less of their pay than almost any other Europeans. Conversely, however, social security benefits are substantial.

Living conditions

Denmark has one of the highest standards of living in the EU and is a clean, green and environmentally conscious country. Prices are generally much higher than in the UK and most new residents find it necessary to budget very carefully at first, despite higher wages. For example, a 250g jar of coffee is £8, a joint of beef £10 per pound. Property prices are low by comparison.

Residence permits

EC nationals do not require work permits. However, a residence permit is required which can be obtained from the **Department for the Supervision of Aliens** (in large towns) or police stations elsewhere. You must also register at the Folkeregisteret in order to use the free national health service, and the Skatteforvattning (tax office) as part of the procedure.

Embassies

Royal Danish Embassy
55 Sloane Street
London SW1X 9SR.
Tel: (020) 7333 0200

Living conditions in Denmark

Living costs	Much higher than UK	
Average 3-bed house	To buy	£95,000
	To rent (month)	£700
Social security system	Deductions from salary are high but sickness/accident/unemployment pay and pensions are generous — normally 100 per cent of your previous salary. Hospital treatment is free to all residents, no insurance scheme is necessary.	
Education	Good. Free to EU nationals	
Standard of living	Very high.	

British Embassy
Kastelsvej 38/40
2100 Copenhagen.
Tel: 264600

Major UK firms in Denmark

Barclays Bank, Beecham, British Steel, Castrol, Fisons, Hoover, ICI, ICL, Rank Xerox, Thorn EMI, United Biscuits.

Language courses

Linguaphone, Carlton Plaza, 111 Upper Richmond Road, London SW15 2TJ. Tel: (020) 83333 4900 Fax: (020) 8333 4883.

Folk High School Information Office, Nytorv 7, 1450 Copenhagen. Tel: 33 3139822 Web: www.folkehojskoler.dk. The Royal Danish Embassy can also advise.

More useful contacts for Denmark

Anglo-Danish Society, 4 Daleside, Gerrards Cross, Bucks. Tel: 01753 884846.

British Council, Møtergade 1, 1116 Copenhagen K. Tel: 33 36 9400.

Danish Bank, 107 Cheapside, London EC2V 6DA. Tel: (020) 7726 6000.

Danish Church, 5 St Katherine's Precincts, London NW1 4HH. Tel: (020) 7935 7584.

Danish Commercial & Technical Translations, 585a Fulham Road, Fulham Broadway, London SW6 5UA. Tel: (020) 7381 0967.

Danish Technical Translation Company, 76 Shoe Lane, London EC4. Tel: (020) 7583 8690.

Danish Translations, 64 Queen Street, London EC4R 1AD. Tel: (020) 7248 8707.

Danish YWCA, 43 Maresfield Gardens, London NW3. Tel: (020) 7435 7232.

Dansk Arbejdsgiverforening (Danish Employers Federation), Vester Voldgade 113, Postboks 386, DK-790 Copenhagen V. Tel: 33 38 90 00. Publishes an English-language guide to employment in Denmark. Web: http://www.da.dk Fax: 33 12 29 76

EASTERN EUROPE

What is the overall potential?

Only in the last ten years have opportunities for living and working in eastern Europe started to become available in significant numbers. Changes in the former Soviet Union, the re-unification of Germany, and a general increase in mutual trust between eastern and western Europe, have at last made it possible, in an area which comprises at least 65 per cent of the land area of the European continent. The countries of the east now firmly recognise that they must develop to survive, and the skills they need can only be recruited in the west.

Only a small proportion of jobs in eastern Europe are career positions offering international wages. Due to a shortage of hard currency most jobs pay modest wages and are done more for the experience than anything else. Many of the positions available are in fact voluntary work.

One advantage is that most eastern European countries are keen to have foreign workers and are very welcoming. Usable skills are almost always required to find a position, but local language ability is not essential.

Main countries with opportunities

- Czech Republic
- Slovak Republic
- Hungary
- Bulgaria
- Poland
- Romania
- Russia
- Latvia
- Lithuania
- Estonia.

Main industries

Most types of industry exist in eastern Europe, as in the west. Most of the industries in eastern Europe, though, are outdated compared with the west. However, some particular activities which are important to the economy of many eastern European countries are:

- vehicle manufacture
- heavy and light engineering

- clothing and textiles
- agriculture
- food processing
- mining/minerals
- iron/steel
- services.

Employment for foreigners

The main categories of work are:

Managerial/financial

Governments and industries require this help to reform and privatise industry and enter world markets. Economists, accountants and those with sound commercial skills may find openings. Opportunities may exist with the EU 'know-how' funds.

Infrastructure

Most of the countries are developing health, public services and transport systems. Jobs are sometimes available with the respective governments or western contractors retained to undertake major projects.

Education/TEFL

Most countries are investing in education, and teaching vacancies are available for qualified and experienced teachers in many countries. Sometimes those not qualified as teachers can find work teaching English as a foreign language.

Voluntary work

Many charities work in eastern Europe and will employ those with skills, especially in education, medicine or technical areas. Work available may be unpaid but sometimes positions do carry modest remuneration.

Most countries do not have any opportunities for unskilled people, or to undertake casual work, as they have large local labour forces.

Finding sources of work

The methods used to find jobs in eastern Europe include:

Newspapers

Some of the quality UK newspapers have vacancies in eastern Europe (see Chapter 2).

Journals

Many professional and executive vacancies appear in UK trade and professional journals (see Chapter 2).

Specialist organisations

Most voluntary work is obtained through specialist organisations in the UK. The following organisations have various projects in eastern Europe:

International Voluntary Service, Old Hall, East Bergholt, Colchester CO7 6TQ. Tel: (01206) 298215 Fax: (01206) 299043.

United Nations Association (Wales), International Youth Service, Temple of Peace, Cathays Park, Cardiff CF10 3AP. Tel: (029) 2022 3088 Fax: (029) 2066 5557.

Christian Outreach, 1 New Street, Leamington Spa CV31 1HP. Tel: (01926) 315301.

Foreign governments/embassies

It is always worth contacting the London embassy of the country you are interested in working in. Sometimes these embassies recruit for government positions, such as in education or health, in strict contrast to western European embassies which do not do this. Some, such as Hungary, will put you in touch with the state employment agency.

Postings

Most of the executive and professional jobs in eastern Europe are obtained as a result of posting from existing jobs. Contracts usually range between three months and one year, rarely longer. It can be a good idea to try to secure a job at home which may later lead to a posting (see Chapter 3).

Speculative methods

Speculative ways of finding a job are not as popular for eastern Europe, but could be worth trying for those with experience and qualifications to offer. Obtain trade directories from the library; embassies can often advise on which directories to use. Poland and the Czech Republic publish a large number of trade directories (see Chapter 2).

Most speculative applications will be to state owned trading corporations, but a number of private trading companies and east-west partnership projects are now starting.

What are working conditions like?

Most westerners are well received in the east and offered firm contracts for a fixed period. Rates of pay will depend on the job and vary from very high to very low. For example, an engineer might earn western rates but a voluntary worker on a hospital refurbishment project might receive £5 per week pocket money. An English teacher in a Hungarian language school might earn £50 a week: excellent by local standards.

The range of benefits can vary. However, most employees should expect accommodation to be provided and health care arrangements made. Executive jobs, and even some voluntary work, both offer an end-of-service bonus. Occasionally, exemption from local taxes is available.

Working hours and contractual details are usually as in the west. However, many people working in the east find that they are willing to work whatever hours are necessary to satisfactorily complete their assignment.

Living conditions

Most countries offer expatriates a reasonable standard of living, assuming that they are in capital cities or other major centres. It is advisable to get local help with such matters as accommodation and transport, as these can be difficult for a foreigner to arrange. Living costs are invariably low and partially compensate for low wages, except if purchasing western goods which are expensive.

Entry regulations

It is necessary to have a work permit to work in all the eastern European countries listed in this section. However, none of them has restrictive immigration policies on the basis that the foreign worker is contributing to their economy.

Full details should be obtained from the embassy of the respective country. Some insist that the permit is obtained from outside their country after a job has been found. Others permit applications to be made within their country. Some states, such as Hungary, waive permit procedures if the employee is working for a western company in partnership with a local company or organisation.

Embassies

Czech Embassy
26 Kensington Palace Gardens
London W8 4QY.
Tel: (020) 7243 1115

Russian Embassy
5 Kensington Palace Gardens
London W8 4QX.
Tel: (020) 7229 3629

Hungarian Embassy
35 Eaton Place
London SW1X 8BY.
Tel: (020) 7235 2664

Bulgarian Embassy
186-188 Queen's Gate
London SW7 5HL.
Tel: (020) 7584 9400

Polish Embassy
73 New Cavendish Street
London W1N 4HQ.
Tel: (020) 7580 0476

Romanian Embassy
4 Palace Green
London W8 4QD.
Tel: (020) 7937 9666

Embassy of the Republic
of Estonia
16 Hyde Park Gate
London SW7 5DG.
Tel: (020) 7589 3428 Email:
tvaravas@estonia.gov.uk

Embassy of Latvia
45 Nottingham Place
London W1M 3FE.
Tel: (020) 7312 0040

Embassy of Lithuania
84 Gloucester Place
London W1H 3HN.
Tel: (020) 7486 6401

FINLAND

What is the overall potential?

Finland generally offers the foreign worker less potential than either Sweden or Norway, neither of which have a large number of vacancies themselves. However, as a less popular country with expatriates, vacancies can be found more easily than elsewhere, assuming that you have suitable skills to offer. Due to lack of career appeal in international circles, Finland sometimes experiences a shortage of experienced and qualified executives and professional people.

Main industries

Finland is much more industrialised than is generally realised. Chief industries include:

- timber and paper products
- engineering
- metal manufacturing

- shipbuilding
- glass
- rubber
- plastics
- chemicals
- textiles and clothing
- electronics
- food processing.

Employment for foreigners

Most opportunities are at a senior level and many personnel are posted; several British companies have branches or subsidiaries in Finland and more are expected to open there as Finland is increasingly seen as a business gateway to Russia.

Casual

Casual work is hard for foreigners to find, and often done on an unofficial basis. Teachers of English are sometimes recruited (it is not always necessary to be qualified) and au pairs, nannies and family helps can often be placed.

Advice to job-hunters

Jobs must be arranged from the UK first as the chance of finding a job on arrival is minimal.

Finding sources of work

There are very few official sources of jobs in Finland. No employment agencies deal with the country on a regular basis. Most jobs will be obtained through speculative applications to addresses in trade directories etc.

Using newspapers

The main newspapers are a useful source of information and can also be used to advertise in. These include *Turun Sanomat* and *Aamulehti*, but *Helsingin Sanomat* is the main one.

Living with a Finnish family

The **Finnish Family Programme** offers native English speaking families the chance to live with a Finnish family for up to a year and teach them English on a casual basis. The system is administered by:

The Ministry of Labour
PO Box 30
00100 Helsinki 10.

In the UK recruitment is handled by:
The Central Bureau for Educational Visits and Exchanges
10 Spring Gardens
London SW1A 2BN.
Tel: (020) 7389 4004.

What are working conditions like?

Working conditions in Finland

Average salary	Executive	£38,000
	Skilled worker	£24,000
Working week	38 hours	
Holiday entitlement	35 days	
Minimum fringe benefits	Similar to Sweden	
Income tax rate	22-42 per cent	
Unemployment rate	3 per cent	
Trade unions	Works organisations are popular.	

Living conditions

Living conditions in Finland

Living costs	Higher than UK	
Average 3-bed house	To buy	£110,500
	To rent (month)	£1,100
Social security system	Benefits are extensive. There is a reciprocal agreement for free or reduced cost medical treatment between the UK and Finland.	
Education	Good	
Standard of living	High. Some parts of Finland are very remote.	

Entry regulations

EU citizens do not require work permits. However, a residence permit is required. This should be obtained from the local police within three months of entry.

Embassies

Finnish Embassy
38 Chesham Place
London SW1X 8HW.
Tel: (020) 7838 6200

British Embassy
Itainen Puistotie 17
00140 Helsinki.
Tel: 9 2286 5100 Fax: 9 2286 5262/5272
Web: http://www.ukembassy.fi/
Email: mailbox@ukembassy.fi

Major UK companies in Finland

Courtaulds, EMI, Fisons, Glaxo, Hoover, ICI, ICL, Pilkington, Rank Xerox, Thorn.

Language courses

Linguaphone, Carlton Plaza, 111 Upper Richmond Road, London SW15 2TJ. Tel: (020) 8333 4900 Fax: (020) 8333 4883.

Finnish for foreigners courses are run by several Finnish universities, notably Helsinki. Further details appear in the booklet *Higher Education in Finland.*

There are also summer courses in Finnish as a foreign language, run at various centres by the Ministry of Education. Other sources of information on these courses are the Ministry of Education, Department for International Relations; and *Finnish Courses*, a news-sheet issued jointly by the Finnish Embassy and the University of London School of Slavonic and East European Studies (it also lists Finnish courses in the UK).

Other useful contacts

British Council, Hakaniemenkatu 2,00530 Helsinki. Tel: 774 3330.
Finlandia Travel Agency Ltd, 227 Regent Street, London W1. Tel: (020) 7409 7334/5.

Finnair, 14 Clifford Street, London W1X 2NS. Tel: (020) 7629 8039.

Finnish Commercial & Technical Translations, 585a Fulham Road, London SW6 5UA. Tel: (020) 7381 0967 Fax: (020) 7381 0960.

Finnish Tourist Board, 30–35 Pall Mall, London SW1Y 5LP. Tel: (020) 7839 4048 Web: http://www.mek.fi

Finnish Translation (Heli Setälä), 136A Tanfield Avenue, Dollis Hill, London NW2 7RR. Tel: (020) 8452 6676 Email: helisetala@compuserve.com

Finnish Institute for International Trade (FINTRA), Kalipintie 2, PO Box 50, 00441 Helsinki. Tel: 3589 228281 Web: www.fintra.fi Email: fintra@fintra.fi

FRANCE

What is the overall potential?

France has some of the best potential for UK workers as French industry is now building many ties with British business and has become involved in UK car manufacture, public utilities, hotels and food processing to mention just a few spheres of interest. Otherwise, France is very protective of national jobs; foreign workers tend to be discouraged, both officially and unofficially, although EU nationals are guaranteed equal rights.

Main industries

French industry divides into two main categories: the largely industrial north of the country (many old, declining industries) and high technology 'sunbelt' areas of the south (Bordeaux, Toulouse, Languedoc and Provence especially). Paris is the major business centre but Lyon is an important commercial city which is often overlooked.

Largest industries are:

- aerospace
- agriculture
- chemicals
- computing
- defence equipment
- food production
- electronics
- motor manufacture
- telecommunications
- tourism.

Employment for foreigners

Executive, professional and skilled

Most foreigners working in France are attracted to either commerce or new, high technology activities (as above) and these are mainly in Paris, Provence or Languedoc. Candidates must be very well skilled/experienced. Secretarial/administrative jobs in Paris are also popular for secretaries/PAs of a high calibre.

Casual

France has good potential for unskilled/casual work, though competition for jobs is tough as young people from all over Europe converge here. Fruit picking (September onwards) is a popular activity but quite hard to find now. Tourism offers some opportunities for campsite couriers (March-September in Brittany or the south) or ski holidays (November-March in the French Alps). France also has good potential for nannies/au pairs.

Advice to job-hunters

Although many French people speak a little English, it is almost essential to speak good French to get most jobs. The French tend to do things to their standards and it helps to be a keen Francophile to succeed here!

Finding sources of work

Jobs can be found from the UK or in France. Qualified personnel stand a good chance of finding work through OPU. Otherwise try private UK employment agencies. Private employment agencies are restricted in France and can largely only handle temporary vacancies. Details of agencies can be found in the French *Yellow Pages (Pages Jaunes)* but the following have offices all over France:

ECCO (Européenne de Commissaires aux Comptes)
11 rue la Boétie
Paris.
Tel: 1 40 07 10 60
Fax: 1 40 07 10 70

Manpower
9 rue Jacques Bingen
75017 Paris.
Tel: 1 44 15 40 40
Fax: 1 44 15 43 33

The state employment service

The French state employment agency is **ANPE** (Agence Nationale pour l'Emploi). ANPE can be unresponsive to letters and phone calls. You can try their web site www.anpe.fr. A list of all ANPEs is available from their head office:

ANPE
10 place de la Défense
92400 Courbevoie.
Tel: 1 46 96 06 50

Using newspapers

French newspapers are a good source of vacancies. The main national ones are *Le Monde, Le Figaro* and *France-Soir.* However, the regional and local press are much more important in France. Main regional newspapers are *Sud-Ouest* (Bordeaux), *La Voix du Nord* (Lille), *Ouest-France* (Rennes), *Le Progrès* (Lyon) and *La Meridional* and *Le Provençal* (Marseille). There are now some English language newspapers in France including *The News, Dordogne Telegraph* and *Riviera Reporter*, all published by:

Universal Media Ltd
75a Marylebone High Street
London W1M 3AR.
Tel: (020) 7935 9134

Executive and professional work

Executive and professional candidates should see French professional journals; details in *Benn's Media Directory International.* Executives could subscribe to the vacancy bulletin called *Courier International*:

146d Poissonniére
75009 Paris.
Tel: 1 53 24 41 67

Making direct applications

Speculative applications can be made direct to employers and can be successful, especially if in French. Addresses can be taken from *Yellow Pages (Pages Jaunes)* which are at all UK libraries. The French Chamber of Commerce in London suggests *Kompass* directory. However, the Franco-British Chamber of Commerce in Paris has a yearbook of members:

31 rue Boissy d'Anglas
75008 Paris.
Tel: 1 53 30 81 30
Fax: 1 53 30 81 35

Work for young people

In addition to other sources, young people seeking casual work can get advice from:

Centre d'Information et de Documentation Jeunesse (CIDJ)
101 quai Branly
75015 Paris.
Tel: 1 44 49 12 00
Fax: 1 40 65 02 61

What are working conditions like?

French employers place great importance on academic qualifications, but personal appearance and integrity are important. Employers are much more relaxed in the south. The importance of being able to speak good French cannot be overestimated; it will command great respect just as a poor knowledge of French may cause some prejudice. French business people tend to mix business and pleasure — another reason for being able to speak the language.

A minimum legal wage exists in France. This is known as the **SMIC** (salaire minimum interprofessionel de croissance). It is reviewed annually.

Working conditions in France

Average salary	Executive	£35,000
	Skilled worker	£24,000
Working week	35-39 hours	
Holiday entitlement	Five weeks plus 11 public holidays	
Minimum fringe benefits	Health benefits and 13th month bonus	
*Income tax rate**	5-56 per cent, average 30 per cent	
Unemployment rate	11 per cent	
Trade unions	Very active especially in public sector	

(*The figure for income tax in each country also includes deductions for social security where appropriate.)

Living conditions

The French place much emphasis on the quality of life. Socialising and entertaining can be an integral part of the business scene. Facilities for sport and recreation are good but rural France can be surprisingly remote.

Living conditions in France	
Living costs	Daily costs slightly higher than UK
Average 3-bed house	To buy £70,000, outside Paris To rent (month) £500, outside Paris
Social security system	Similar benefits to UK, but paid at higher rates. Hospital treatment is not free and either state or private health insurance is essential.
Education	Good. Free to EU nationals.
Standard of living	High in cities/towns but rural areas can be surprisingly backward.

Residence permits

EU nationals do not require work permits but do require a residence permit, called a **Carte de Séjour**. This should be obtained within three months of arriving, at the local mairie or préfecture in the area where you intend to live.

Embassies

French Embassy
58 Knightsbridge
London SW1X 7JT.
Tel: (020) 01 1000
Email: press@ambafrance.org.uk
Fax: (020) 7201 1004
Web: http://www.ambafrance.org.uk

British Embassy
35 rue de Faubourg St Honoré
75383 Paris.
Tel: 1 44 51 31 00
Web: http://www.amb-grandebretagne.fr/

Consulates in Bordeaux, Lille, Lyon and Marseille.

Major UK companies in France

Barclays Bank, British Steel, British Aerospace, Commercial Union, Courtaulds, Guardian Royal, ICI, ICL, National Westminster Bank, Lloyds Bank, Lucas, Marks & Spencer, Rover, Rowntree Mackintosh, Standard Chartered Bank, Thorn EMI, Wimpey Construction.

Summer and work camp opportunities

Summer camps

There are well over 20,000 summer camps in France each year held for children and teenagers. Foreigners seeking paid work as counsellors in these camps normally need the BAFA Certificate (**Brevet d'Aptitude aux Fonctions d'Animateur**). For further information contact:

ANSTJ, Association Nationale Sciences et Techniques Jeunesse, 16 place Jacques Brel, 91130 Ris-Orangis. Tel: 1 69 02 76 10.

CEMEA, Centre d'Entrainement aux Méthodes d'Education Active, 24 rue Marc Séguin, 75883 Paris. Tel: 1 53 26 24 24.

CPCV, Comité Protestant des Centres de Vacances, 47 rue de Clichy, 75311 Paris. Tel: 1 42 80 06 99.

STAJ, 3 rue de Metz, 75010 Paris. Tel: 1 42 46 67 97.

UCPA, Union Nationale de Centres Sportifs et de Plein Air, 28 bd de Sébastopol, 75004 Paris Cedex 13. Tel: 1 48 04 76 76.

UFVC, Union Française des Centres de Vacances,10 quai de la Charente, 75019 Paris. Tel: 1 44 72 14 14.

Work camps

These can be a lot of fun — if hard work — offering summer jobs for volunteers in all kinds of French work camps doing everything from archaeological digs to environmental conservation. The best known organisations include:

Alpes de Lumière, Prieuré de Salagon, Mane, 04300 Forcalquier. Tel: 92 75 70 50 Fax: 92 75 70 51.

Concordia,1 rue de Metz, 75010 Paris. Tel: 1 45 23 00 23 Fax: 01 47 70 68 27.

Etudes et Chantiers, 3 rue des Petits Gras, Delegation Internationale UNAREC, Clermont-Ferrand 63000. Tel: 4 73 36 52 28.

Jeunesse et Reconstruction, 10, rue de Trévise, 75009 Paris. Tel: 1 47 70 15 88.

Mouvement de la Paix, 94 rue Jean Pierre Tïmbaud, 75011 Paris. Tel: 1 43 14 04 18.

Neige et Merveilles, 06430 Saint-Dalmas-de-Tende. Tel: 93 04 62 40 or 93 97 10 39.

Language courses

Berlitz, 9–13 Grosvenor Street, London W1A 3BZ. Tel: (020) 7915 0909.
In Paris: Tel: 1 40 74 00 17.

Inlingua, 28 Rotton Park Road, Birmingham B16 9JL. Tel: (0121) 454 0204.

Inlingua, 109 rue de l'Université, 75007 Paris. Tel: 45 511 46 60 Fax. 1 45 55 85 46.

Linguaphone, Carlton Plaza, 111 Upper Richmond Road, London SW15 2TJ. Tel: 0800 282417.

Alliance Française, 110 boulevard Raspail, 75270 Paris. Tel: 1 45 44 38 28.

Alliance Française, 1 Dorset Square, London NW1 6PU. Tel: (020) 7723 6439.

Institut Français, 14 Cromwell Place, London SW7 2JN. Tel: (020) 7581 2701.

Information on many more courses is available from the French Embassy Cultural Section, 23 Cromwell Road, London SW7 2EL. Tel: (020) 7838 2055.

More useful contacts

Travel (UK addresses)

Air France, Terminal 2 London Heathrow Airport, Hounslow, Middlesex TW6 1EU. Tel: (020) 8759 2311 (offices also in Birmingham, Manchester and Glasgow).

Brittany Ferries, Millbay Docks, Plymouth PL1 3EW. Tel: 0870 5360360.

French Government Tourist Office, 178 Piccadilly, London W1V 0AL. Tel: 0891 244123 Fax: (020) 7493 6594 Email: info@mdlf.co.uk

French Railways House, 179 Piccadilly, London W1V 0BA. Tel: 0870 5848848.

Travel (French addresses)

Automobile Club d'Ile de France, 6 place de la Concorde, 75008 Paris. Tel: 1 43 12 43 12.

Centre d'Information et de Documentation Jeunesse (CIDJ), 101 quai Branly, 75740 Paris Cedex 15.

Centre d'Information Jeunesse (CIJ), 1 Parvis de la Préfecture/1 place des Arts, BP315, 95000 Cergy-Pointoise Cedex. Tel: 1 34 41 67 67 Fax: 1 30 38 91 00.

Centre National des Oeuvres Universitaires et Scolaires (National Centre for University and School Activities), 6 rue Jean Calvin, 75005 Paris. Tel: 1 55 43 58 58 Email: infodoc@cnous.fr

Châteaux et Hôtels de France, 12 rue Auber, 75009 Paris. Tel: 1 40 07 00 20 Fax: 1 40 07 00 30.

Organisation pour la tourisme universitaire (OTU), 39 Avenue Georges Bernanos, 75005 Paris. Will issue a FIYTO card to under 26s (Federation of International Youth Travel Organisations). Tel: 1 44 41 38 50 Fax: 1 46 33 19 98.

SNCF Central Information service (French Railways). Tel: 8 36 35 35 35.

Syndicats d'Initiative. The network of French tourist bureaux found in most towns.

Syndicat d'Initiative de Paris, 127 avenue des Champs Elysées, 75008 Paris. Tel: 8 36 68 31 12 Fax: 1 49 52 53 00 Email: info@paris-tourist.com

Touring Club de France, Port Champs Elysées, 75008 Paris. Tel: 1 42 65 90 70.

Accommodation

Association pour le Logement des Jeunes Travailleurs, 115 rue Ferrus, 75014 Paris. Tel: 1 44 16 94 00.

Comité Nationale des Unions Chrétiennes de Jeunes Gens (YMCA), Résidence Sienne, 5 place de Venetie, 75013 Paris. Tel: 1 45 83 62 63.

Confédération des Maisons de Jeunes et de la Culture, 168 bis, rue Cardinet, 75017 Paris. Tel: 1 44 35 29 50 Fax: 1 42 29 01 44.

Fédération Française des Maisons de Jeunes et de la Culture, 15 rue La Condamine, 75017 Paris. Tel: 1 44 69 82 25 Fax: 1 44 69 82 30.

Fédération Unie des Auberges de Jeunesse (FUAJ), boutique Jules Ferry, 4 boulevard Jules Ferry, 75011 Paris. Tel: 1 43 57 43 28 Fax: 1 43 57 53 90. Will issue an International Youth Hostel Card.

Fondation Nationale de la Cité Universitaire, 19 boulevard Jordan, 75014 Paris. Tel: 1 45 88 75 56. Campus accommodation for foreign university students.

Ligue Française des Auberges de Jeunesse, 67 rue Vergniaud, 75073

Paris. Tel: 1 44 16 78 78 Fax: 1 44 16 78 80.

Office du Tourisme Universitaire (OTU), 39 Avenue Georges Bernanos, 75005 Paris. Tel: 1 44 41 38 50 Fax: 1 46 33 19 98.

Union de Centres de Recontres Internationales de France (UCRIF), 27 rue Turbigo, 75002 Paris. Tel: 1 40 26 57 64 Fax: 1 40 26 58 20.

Union des Foyers de Jeunes Travailleurs (UFJT), 12 avenue Général de Gaulle, 94300 Vincennes. Tel: 1 41 74 81 00. Hostel accommodation for 18-25 year olds with jobs or training placements. Advance booking usually necessary.

Cultural, educational and social

Association for the Study of Modern and Contemporary France, University of Bath, Bath BA2 7AY. Tel: (01225) 826826. For French teachers and researchers.

British Council, 9 rue Constantine, 75007 Paris. Tel: 1 49 55 73 00 Fax: 1 47 05 77 02.

British Institute in Paris, 9 rue Constantine, 75007 Paris. Tel: 1 44 11 73 70.

Centre Regional des Oeuvres Universitaires et Scolaires (CROUS), 39 avenue Georges Bernanos, 75005 Paris. Tel: 1 43 29 20 75.

Council of International Educational Exchange, 1 place Odéon, 75006 Paris. Tel: 1 44 41 74 74 Fax: 1 43 26 97 45. Can provide a student ID card qualifying for a wide variety of concessions.

Franco-British Society, Room 636, Linen Hall, 162-168 Regent Street, London W1R 5TB. Tel: (020) 7734 0815. Exists to encourage British understanding of French artistic, scientific, social and economic achievements, through travel, personal contacts and meetings. Publishes a journal twice a year. Membership includes individuals and firms. Established in 1944.

Franco-Scottish Society, Traquair, Innerleithen EH44 6PU. Tel: (01896) 831227 Fax: (01896) 831227. An old-established (1895) organisation founded to promote Franco-Scottish friendship. It has several local branches.

Ministère de l'Education Nationale, 110 rue de Grenelle, 75007 Paris. Tel: 1 55 55 10 10.

Society for French Studies, Department of French, University of Nottingham, Nottingham NG7 2RD. An organisation of some 1,700 individual members and organisations, it exists to promote French studies in higher education in Britain and the Commonwealth. It publishes a quarterly journal (*French Studies*).

YWCA,7 rue Auguste Vacquerie, 75116 Paris. Tel: 1 47 20 44 02.

Business contacts in Britain

DATAR, 21-24 Grosvenor Place, London SW1X 7HU. Tel: (020) 8823 1895. The French industrial development agency which produces information on a wide variety of French commercial matters.

French Embassy (Financial Counsellor). Tel: (020) 7201 1066.

Overseas Trade Division, Department of Trade and Industry, 1 Victoria Street, London SW1H 0ET. Tel: (020) 7215 4080 (French country desk).

Business contacts in France

Barclays Bank SA, 81 av Victor Hugo, 75116 Paris. Tel: 1 53 64 10 10 Fax: 1 40 67 93 54. Also: 6 Rond Point des Champs Elysées, 75008 Paris. Tel: 1 44 95 13 80 Fax: 1 45 44 54 61. 24 ave Kléber, 75016 Paris. Tel: 1 44 17 89 89 Fax: 1 45 00 24 66.

British Embassy, 35 rue Faubourg St Honoré, 75383 Paris. The Financial and Commercial Counsellor, Tel: 1 44 51 31 00. There are branches of the Commercial Section in Bordeaux, Lille, Lyon and Marseille.

Centre Français du Commerce Extérieur (French Centre for Foreign Trade), 10 avenue d'Iéna, 75116 Paris. Tel: 1 40 73 34 60 Fax: 1 40 73 31 46.

DATAR, 1 avenue Charles Floquet, 75007 Paris. Tel: 1 40 65 12 34. The French industrial development agency.

Franco-British Chamber of Commerce and Industry, 31 rue Boissy d'Anglas, 75008 Paris. Tel: 1 53 30 81 30 Fax: 1 53 30 81 35. Publishes a monthly journal *Cross Channel Trade*. The Chamber also has offices in Marseille, Merignac, Lille, Le Havre, Lyon, Rouen, Cherbourg, Strasbourg and Nice. It is able to provide a wide variety of commercial information, details of trade and professional bodies, contacts, reception and interview facilities (for a fee), and runs a Junior Section for business people aged up to 40.

Lloyds Bank SA, 15 avenue d'léna, 75016 Paris Cedex 16. Tel: 1 44 43 42 41 Fax: 1 44 43 42 40.

Further reading on France

Bottin Administratif, 141 Rue de Javel, Paris. Business Registers. Editions Techniques et Scientifiques.

Dyson, Henry, *Buying and Selling Your Home in France* (Sweet & Maxwell 1991) 2nd edition, 208pp.

France: World of Information (Mercury Business Books 1992) 160pp.

Hart, Alan, *Living & Working in France* (How To Books 1998) 208pp.

Hampshire, David, *Buying a Home in France* (Survival Books 1999) 238pp.

Kompass France, 66 Quai Mar Joffre 92415 Courbevoie, Paris, France. Web: *http://www.kompass.fr*. A comprehensive industrial directory giving company data for most firms in France.

Scholey, Andrew, *French Homes for the British* (Wisefile 1990). 162pp, illustrated paperback.

Taxation in France (Pannell Kerr Forster 1999). 176pp, paperback.

GERMANY

What is the overall potential?

Since the 1950s Germany experienced a skills shortage and always needed skilled workers from abroad to fill vacancies in this successful industrial country; six million of Germany's 90 million inhabitants are foreigners. Since reunification, however, this demand has fallen considerably as workers from former East Germany and eastern Europe can now be recruited. However, UK workers are favoured in Germany due to their good reputation for hard work. The German economy remains one of the most successful in the world so future employment potential is good.

Main industries

Germany has most types of industry that exist in any advanced country. They are usually very prosperous; declining industries are few but include:

- coal
- shipbuilding
- steel.

Key industries are:

- engineering
- electrical manufacturing
- motor manufacture
- aerospace
- electronics
- computing
- telecommunications
- chemicals.

Employment for foreigners

Executive, professional and skilled
Many people who go to work in Germany do so in a professional/executive capacity in the key industries (as above). Standards demanded in business/commerce are very high indeed. In addition, British people will be considered for most middle-ranking professional and technical jobs. Engineers, technicians and teachers will find that most German cities have a range of vacancies. Construction workers are still recruited (often via the Netherlands) but must be qualified and well experienced.

Casual
Casual jobs are usually fairly easy to find in Germany, as many Germans will not do dirty or boring work, but there is competition with Turkish immigrant workers (*gastarbeiter*) for this. Most vacancies occur in shops, warehouses, hotels, catering establishments and cleaning — all popular with young working travellers.

Advice to job-hunters

Although now reunited, job-seekers should confine their search mainly to the former West Germany. Opportunities in the former East Germany are few, wages are lower and unemployment substantial. Most former East German industries are no longer viable but West German industry is investing there at a quickening pace.

Finding sources of work

Jobs can be found both from UK or on arrival in Germany. Qualified personnel stand a very good chance of finding work through OPU. Otherwise try private UK agencies which are especially active in technical/engineering industries. Private employment agencies are restricted by law in Germany; some temporary employment bureaux, such as Manpower, can be located via the *Yellow Pages (Gelbe Seiten)*.

The state employment service
The German state employment service is **Arbeitsamt**. It is extremely efficient and very willing to help foreigners with suitable skills. Call in person to an office, which are in all main towns. A special agency, Zentralstelle für Arbeitsvermittlung, will deal with written enquiries about jobs from abroad and can find jobs for suitable people. The address is:

ZAV
Villemombler Strasse 76
53123 Bonn.
Tel: 0228 - 7130
Fax: 0228 - 7131111

Using newspapers
German newspapers are a good source of vacancies. The main ones are *Frankfurter Allgemeine Zeitung* and *Die Welt*. Also see *Süddeutsche Zeitung* and *Bayernkurier* (Munich), *Kölnische Rundschau* (Cologne), *Weser Kurier* (Bremen), *Stuttgarter Zeitung* (Stuttgart). Although the capital, the Berlin press, such as *Berliner Morgenpost*, carries rather less weight than the other papers.

Executive and professional work
Executive and professional applicants who speak some German should refer to professional journals for the top jobs. Also see specialist vacancy bulletins which include *Markt+Chance*, published by ZAV (above) and:

Position
Postfach 1455
D-82317 Starnberg.
Tel: 08151 7710
Fax: 08151 71190

Making direct applications
Speculative applications can be made direct to employers and applications in English can sometimes be successful. Addresses can be obtained from the *Yellow Pages (Gelbe Seiten)* which are at all main UK libraries.

The German Chamber of Industry and Commerce
16 Buckingham Gate
London SW1E 6LB.
Tel: (020) 7976 4100
Fax: (020) 7976 4101
Email: mail@ahk-london.co.uk
Web: http://www.ahk-london.co.uk

has a membership directory with useful addresses. Door-knocking can be quite successful for working travellers.

Work for young people
Young people seeking casual work should contact Arbeitsamt and ZAV.

What are working conditions like?

Germans work hard and employers can be very demanding, but evenings and weekends are sacrosanct. Business and pleasure are never mixed. Business methods are efficient and formal. Colleagues rarely use first names even after many years and do not socialise.

Living conditions

Germans live a very regimented way of life. Everything is done by the book, rules and regulations and bureaucracy abound. People can be very formal but underneath they are usually friendly. Many have a special regard for the British whom they consider, like themselves, superior to other Europeans.

Working conditions in Germany

Average salary	Executive	£44,000
	Skilled worker	£24,000
Working week	40 hours	
Holiday entitlement	24 days minimum, may receive 42 days	
Minimum fringe benefits	13th month bonus and at least 50 per cent of health insurance premiums paid	
Income tax rate	19.5-56 per cent	
Unemployment rate	9 per cent	
Trade unions	Active only in older industries	

Living conditions in Germany

Living costs	Daily costs slightly higher than UK	
Average 3-bed house	To buy	£115,000
	To rent (month)	£900
Social security system	Similar benefits to UK, but paid at higher rates. Hospital treatment is not free and either state or private health insurance is essential.	
Education	Very good. Free to EU nationals.	
Standard of living	Very high, often better than UK.	

Residence permits

EU nationals do not need a work permit but must still have a residence permit, known as an **Aufenthaltsgenehmigung**. Apply for this within three months of arrival at the Ausländeramt, which is usually in the local Rathaus (town hall).

A **health certificate** will be required for those working in catering trades. Obtain this at the local **Gesundheitsamt**.

Embassies

German Embassy
23 Belgrave Square
London SW1X 0PZ.
Tel: (020) 7824 1300
Email: mail@german-embassy.org.uk
Web: http://www.german-embassy.org.uk

British Embassy
Unter den Linden 32-24
D-10117 Berlin.
Tel: 030-201 840
Fax: 030-201 84158
Email: astrid.ladd@berlin.mail.sco.gov.uk
Web: http://www.britischebotschaft.de

Major UK companies in Germany

Barclays Bank, Beecham Group, Boots, BAT, Cable & Wireless, Cadbury Schweppes, Croda, EMI, GKN, ICL, Lloyds Bank, Marconi, Rank Xerox, Shell, Vickers.

German language courses

Berlitz, 9–13 Grosvenor Streett, London W1A 3BZ. Tel: (020) 7915 0909. In Heidelberg tel: (06221) 164004.

Inlingua, 28 Rotton Park Road, Birmingham B16 9JL. Tel: (0121) 454 0204.

Inlingua, Waisenhausplatz 28, Postfach 171428, 3001 Bern. Tel: 031 311 2413 Fax: 031 311 0240.

Linguaphone, Carlton Plaza, 111 Upper Richmond Road, London SW15 2TJ. Tel: 0800 282417.

Deutsch in Deutschland, Hauptstrasse 26, 63811 Stockstadt/Main.

Information on courses run by the Goethe-Institut is available from 50 Princes Gate, Exhibition Road, London SW7 2PH. Tel: (020) 7596 4000.

More useful contacts

Allgemeiner Deutsche Automobil Club (ADAC), D-81373 München, Westpark 8, Germany. Tel: 089 76760 Fax: 089 76762500 Web: http://www.adac.de

Automobilclub von Deutschland (AVD), D-60528 Frankfurt, Lyonerstrasse 16, Germany. Tel: 0049 069 66060 Fax: 069 6606 789.

British Chamber of Commerce in Germany (BCCG), D-50678 Köln, Severinstrasse 60, Germany.

British Consulates-General:

40476 Düsseldorf, Yorckstrasse 19, Germany. Tel: 0211 94480 Fax: 0211 488190.

60323 Frankfurt am Main, Bockenheimer Landstrasse 42, Germany. Tel: 069 170 002 Fax: 069 729 553 Web: www.britischebotschaft.de

20148 Hamburg, Harvestehuderweg 8a, Germany. Tel: 040 448032 0 Fax: 040 41 7259.

80538 München Bürkleinstrasse 10, Germany. Tel: 089 21109-0 Fax: 089 21109-144.

British-German Association, 18 Conduit Street, London W1R 9TD. Tel: (020) 7629 4975. Subscription for single members £10, for married couples £16. Has a full programme of events including a Youth Programme.

British Overseas Trade Board, Germany Desk, Room 374, 1 Victoria Street, London SW1H 0LT.

Deutsches Jugendherbergswerk Hauptverband (Youth Hostel Association), D-32756 Detmold, Bülowstrasse 26, Germany. Tel: 052 31 74010 Web: www.djh.de

German Academic Exchange Service, 34 Belgrave Square, London SW1X 8QB. Tel: (020) 7235 1736. 53175 Bonn 2, Kennedyallee 50, Germany.

German Airlines Lufthansa, London Heathrow Airport, Hounslow, Middlesex TW6 2RD. Tel: 0845 7737747.

German Broadcasting, 10 Great Chapel Street, London W1. Tel: (020) 7439 7460.

German Embassy, 23 Belgrave Square, London SW1X 8PZ. Tel: (020) 7824 1300.

German National Tourist Office, Nightingale House, 65 Curzon Street, London W1. Tel: (020) 7493 0080.

German Travel Bureau (DER), 18 Conduit Street, London W1. Tel (020) 7408 0111 Fax: (020) 7629 7442.

Goethe Institut, 50 Princes Gate, Exhibition Road, London SW7 2PH. Tel: (020) 7596 4000. The German cultural organisation which provides German language classes and other facilities.

Further reading on Germany

General

AA Explorer: Germany (AA Publishing 2000).

Aldridge, Janet, *Off the Beaten Track: Germany* (Moorland Publishing, 1993).

Ardagh, John, *Germany and the Germans* (Penguin 1995).

Bentley, James, *Germany* (Blue Guide) (A & C Black 1995).

Berlin Guide (Metropolis International Ltd. 2000).

Berlin Transit: A Travel Guide 1986-7 (Thomas Cook 1986).

Berlitz Travel Guide to Berlin (Berlitz Guides 1995).

Bernhard, Marianne, *Baedeker's AA Berlin* (Automobile Association 1998).

Brown, K., *Germany: Charming Inns & Itineraries* (Fodor 2000).

Craig, Gordon A., *The Germans* (Penguin 1996).

Cunningham, N. & D. Peterson, *Germany* (Duncan Peterson Publishing 2000).

Diel, A. & J. Payne, *German Wine Guide* (Abbeville Press 1999).

Hall, Christine, *How to Live & Work in Germany* (How To Books, 2nd edition 1995).

Horvath, G. *How to Eat Out in Germany* (Gremese Paperback 1999).

Hurst, M. *A Flavour of Germany* (Hodder Wayland 1999).

Insight Guides: Germany (APA Publications 1999).

Let's Go 2000: Germany (Pan Paperback 1999).

McLachlen, G. *Germany: The Rough Guide* (Rough Guide 1998).

Steves, R. *Rick Steves' Germany, Austria & Switzerland: 1999* (John Muir Publications 1999).

GREECE

What is the overall potential?

Greece is one of the poorer EU countries and, as such, has not attracted a lot of professional expatriates so far. The potential should improve in future, although Greece has not developed industrially to the same extent as Spain since joining the EU. Many casual workers are attracted to the islands in the summer, but comparatively few find reliable opportunities and pay is always low.

Main industries

Greece has two dominant industries employing 68 per cent of the workforce:

- agriculture
- tourism.

Most agriculture is small-scale but cotton, vegetables and wine production are substantial. Large industries include:

- food processing
- textiles and clothing
- chemicals
- engineering
- mineral exploitation.

Shipping and transport is a major Greek industry.

Employment for foreigners

Executive and professional

Executives and professionals mainly work only in Athens. This city serves as a gateway to the Middle East and South East Europe and most of the jobs are connected with this rather than with domestic Greek industry. Expatriates in Athens are largely employed in:

- journalism, the media and advertising
- shipping
- international trade
- banking and finance
- textile production industries
- mining/minerals.

Casual

Casual jobs can be taken anywhere and Greek employers are always keen to take on casual help at busy times, though for low pay. TEFL teachers (not necessarily qualified) may find work in Athens, as might au pairs and nannies. Rural Greece offers plenty of work in the fields and fruit picking but this can be extremely hard for low pay.

Work for young people

In summer the islands will take on young people to work in bars, discos, nightclubs, etc but there is usually a surplus of job-hunters. British holiday companies recruit a fairly small number of staff to work in Greece.

Advice to job-hunters

Apart from some specialist professionals, Greece is hardly yet a career destination. It mostly attracts working travellers, not all of whom find any or adequate work. It is not usually necessary to speak Greek for many professional and most casual jobs.

Finding sources of work

Jobs can be found from the UK or in Greece but it can be easier to be on the spot. Contacts are so important and organised methods offer only a limited chance of success. No private UK employment agencies are known to deal with Greece. Private employment agencies are numerous in Athens (not all are reputable), see details in *Yellow Pages*. One which does recruit UK staff, both skilled and unskilled, is:

Athenian Agency
PO Box 51181
14510 Kifissia.
Tel: 01 808 1005

The Greek state employment agency is not easy for foreigners to use.

Using newspapers

Greek newspapers are difficult to understand, but there are two English language newspapers which are good for casual work and advertising Situations Wanted. These are:

Athens News
Christou Lada 3
Athens 10237
Tel: (+301) 333355
Fax: (+301) 3231384
Web: http://www.athensnews.dolnet.gr

and

Greek Daily Courier
37 M Alexandrou St.,
Lárisa.
Fax: 041 250762

Executives should see international professional journals, especially those published in Germany, for Greek vacancies.

Making direct applications

Speculative applications are the very best way of finding work in Greece — it is often necessary to talk oneself into a job! Many English language teaching institutes and tourist facilities recruit this way. Make phone calls, write letters or, preferably, call in person. Addresses can be taken from *Yellow Pages* (or the *Blue Pages* English version) and trade directories like *Kompass*.

The British Hellenic Chamber of Commerce
25 Vas Sofias Ave
GR-10674 Athens.
Tel: 30(1) 72 10 361
Fax: 30(1) 72 18 751
can supply a list of members. Village cafes and, in Athens, youth hostels, are often unofficial job agencies for casual work.

What are working conditions like?

Many jobs in Greece are 'unofficial'. Labour legislation is incomplete and word-of-mouth agreements more usual than contracts. Pay is low, hours are often 'as necessary' and some employers are dishonest in this regard. Women may find it hard to get work, except in bars, cleaning, etc. Executives should be able to demand good contracts.

Working conditions in Greece

Average salary	Executive	£22,000
	Skilled worker	£10,550
Working week	44 hours, but varies	
Holiday entitlement	21 days, plus 12 public holidays	
Minimum fringe benefits	Few, but executives may be offered a housing allowance, car, school fees and relocation benefits.	
Income tax rate	8-50 per cent, average 35 per cent	
Unemployment rate	11 per cent	
Trade unions	Active, but expatriates rarely participate.	

Living conditions

Greece offers a relaxed way of life and some areas can be remote. Athens is chaotic, dirty and hot in summer but offers most facilities and is a very cosmopolitan city. Standards of property and most services are lower than would be found elsewhere in the EU.

Residence permits

EU nationals do not require a work permit, but must have a residence permit to stay longer than three months. This can be obtained from the

Living conditions in Greece

Living costs	Daily costs lower than UK
Average 3-bed house	To buy £65, 000, outside resorts To rent (month) £400, outside resorts
Social security system	A basic system of unemployment insurance, sickness benefits and pensions exists with contributions to IKA deducted from wages. Hospital treatment free if registered, but poor in some places and many expatriates take private health insurance.
Education	Free to EU nationals, but of variable standard. British schools are available in Athens.
Standard of living	Modest in most places, some areas and islands are fairly primitive and remote.

police station or, in Athens, the **Aliens Department** of the **Ministry of Public Order**.

Embassies

Embassy of Greece
1a Holland Park
London W11 3TP.
Tel: (020) 7229 3850

British Embassy
1 Ploutarchou Street
10675 Athens.
Tel: (+301) 7272600
Web: http://www.british-embassy.gr

Major UK companies in Greece

Barclays Bank, BP, Commercial Union, EMI, General Accident, Glaxo, ICL, ICI, Legal & General, Lucas, Midland Bank, National Westminster Bank, Royal Bank of Scotland, Shell.

Language courses

Linguaphone, Carlton Plaza, 111 Upper Richmond Road, London SW15 2TJ. Tel:(020) 8333 4900 Fax: (020) 8333 4883.

Dept. International Relations, University of Athens, 30 Panepistimou St., 10679 Athens. Fax: (+301) 3602145

Information on other organisations which run courses in modern Greek is available from the Greek Embassy.

Useful contacts for Greece

The Greek Bookshop (Zeno), 6 Denmark Street, London WC2H 8LP. Tel: (020) 7836 2522.

Greek Embassy School, 3 Pierpoint Road, London W3. Tel: (020) 8992 6156.

Greek Islands Sailing Club, 10–12 Upper Square, Old Isleworth, Middlesex TW7 7BJ. Tel: (020) 8232 9780.

Greek Translations, 31 Athenaeum Road, London N20 9AL. Tel: (020) 8445 3224.

Greek Translations, 64 Queen Street, London EC4. Tel: (020) 7248 8707.

Hellenic Book Service, 91 Fortress Road, London NW5 1AG. Tel: (020) 7267 9499.

How to Live & Work in Greece, Peter Reynolds (How To Books 1996).

National Tourist Organisation of Greece, 4 Conduit Street, London W1. Tel: (020) 7734 5997.

Contacts in Greece

British Council, 17 Kolonaki Square, 10673 Athens. Tel: (+301) 3692333 Fax: (+301) 3634769 Email: british.council@britcoun.gr Web: http://www.britcoun.gr

British-Hellenic Chamber of Commerce, 25 Vas. Sofias, 10674 Athens. Tel: (+301) 721 0361 Fax: (+301) 721 8751.

Coopers and Lybrand, Accountants, Abacus House, 9 Semitlou Street, 11528 Athens. Tel: (+301) 77 10 112.

ETBA (The Greek Investment Bank), 87 Sygroy Ave, 11745 Athens. Tel: (+301) 9242900 Fax: (+301) 9241513. Produces an investment guide to Greece with a labour law chapter. The guide is updated every two or three years, and is written for ETBA by the Greek office of Coopers & Lybrand. Web: http://www.etba.gr Email: news@ebta.gr

Ministry of Labour, 40 Piraeus Street, Athens. Tel: (+301) 529 5001.

OAED (the state manpower and job placement agency), Ethinihis Antistasis 8 Str., 16610 Glyfada. Tel: (+301) 9989000 Web: http://www.oaed.gr

IRELAND (REPUBLIC OF)

What is the overall potential?

For many years Ireland has been known as an area of overall emigration, with Irish people going to live and work in all parts of the world, including the UK. However, the traffic is most certainly two-way and, due to the English-speaking connection, it is usually British people who have first call on the jobs which are suitable for foreigners.

Although a small country the Irish economy has boomed in recent years and this has led to a labour shortage in certain specialist industries.

Main industries

The main Irish industries are well developed and advanced and, in many cases, well geared to serving export markets. Key areas include mineral exploitation, fisheries, forestry, agriculture, textiles, food processing and electrical manufacture. Key service activities include financial services, transport (especially air and sea) and utilities. Tourism also contributes to the economy.

Employment for foreigners

Foreigners who speak English find that they can take any job in Ireland. British workers are found in all sectors, but especially at executive or skilled worker level, and are predominant in the finance and food processing industries to name but two. It is quite difficult to obtain casual or unskilled work as unemployment in these sectors is high. For example, little work is available in summer tourism.

Advice to job-hunters

Most jobs call for fluency in English. A knowledge of the Gaelic language is unnecessary.

The main employment opportunities for foreigners are in the capital city of Dublin and, possibly, Cork. Job opportunities outside these areas are few in number.

Finding sources of work

All the main methods of finding work can be tried. Due to the lack of a language barrier it is usually easier to make an exploratory trip to Ireland to investigate the possibilities. Refer to the *FRES Yearbook* and *CEPEC Guide* for details of UK agencies dealing with Ireland. However, it may be simpler to contact Irish employment agencies direct. A list can be obtained from the *Yellow Pages* (called *Golden Pages*) or by writing to the Department of Enterprise, Trade and Employment, Kildare Street, Dublin 2. Tel: 01 6312121.

The Irish state employment service is known as FÁS (Foras Áiseanna Saothair). All main towns have a FÁS office and these are listed in the telephone directory.

Using newspapers

The main newspapers are *The Irish Independent* (see Thursday for most job advertisements), *The Irish Times* (see Friday) and *The Irish Press*. Also see regional newspapers. Some executive jobs are advertised in UK newspapers, such as *The Guardian* and *The Independent* and also UK professional journals.

Making direct applications

It is worth considering making speculative applications and the Irish way of doing business is particularly suited to telephone and personal calls. Information on companies may be obtained from:

The Chamber of Commerce of Ireland
22 Merrion Square
Dublin 2
Tel: 01 661 2888
Fax: 01 6612811
Email: Chambers@iol.ie

Dublin Chamber of Commerce
7 Clare Street
Dublin 2.
Tel: 01 6130800
Email: info@dubchamber.ie

What are working conditions like?

Working conditions vary between those in small, family businesses where standards and terms and conditions of employment may be below UK standards and larger companies where they are equivalent or higher. More emphasis is placed on training than in the UK. Minimum wages apply to some sectors.

Living conditions

The standard of living is similar to that in the UK in towns and cities,

Working conditions in Ireland		
Average salary	Executive	£24,500
	Skilled worker	£16,300
Working week	38-42 hours	
Holiday entitlement	15 days, but most receive more	
Minimum fringe benefits	Similar to UK	
Income tax rate	35-38 per cent	
Unemployment rate	16 per cent	
Trade unions	Up to 75 per cent membership in some industries.	

Living conditions in Ireland		
Living costs	Slightly higher than UK	
Average 3-bed house	To buy	£55,000
	To rent (month)	£500
Social security system	A wide range of benefits is provided under the PRSI (Pay Related Social Insurance) scheme to which all employees must contribute.	
Education	Free and of a good standard.	
Standard of living	Comparable with UK in urban areas.	

but usually lower in rural districts. Property is slightly cheaper but some other living costs (fuel, entertainment etc) are greater. The cultural differences between the UK and Ireland should not be underestimated.

Residence permits

EU nationals do not require a work permit. However, British citizens wishing to work in Ireland should possess a full UK passport.

Embassies

Embassy of the Republic of Ireland
17 Grosvenor Place
London SW1X 7HR
Tel: (020) 7235 2171.

British Embassy
29 Merrion Road
Ballsbridge
Dublin 4.
Tel: 01 205 3742
Fax: 01 205 3893
Email: bembassy@internet-ireland.ie
Web: www.britishembassy.ie

Useful contacts for the Irish Republic

Aer Lingus, 83 Staines Road, Hounslow, Middlesex TW3 3JB. Tel: (020) 8234 4333.
The Irish Club, 82 Eaton Square, London SW1. Tel: (020) 7235 4164.
Irish Independent Newspapers Ltd, 76 Shoe Lane, London EC4. Tel: (020) 7353 4325.
The Irish Times, 76 Fleet Street, London EC4. Tel: (020) 7353 8981.
Irish Tourist Board, Ireland House, 150 New Bond Street, London W1. Tel: (020) 7493 3201.

ITALY

What is the overall potential?

Italy has always tended to have a rather insular outlook when it comes to expatriate employment; few foreigners are recruited, and national jobs are jealously guarded both by employers and the Government, which has implemented fewer EU directives than any EU country and which imposes stiff bureaucracy on foreign employment. Italy is somewhat impoverished in the south, but rich and prosperous in the north where most executives work, especially around Milan and Turin and the Italian lakes.

Main industries

Most industries operate in Italy. Major employers are in:

- engineering
- motor manufacture
- iron/steel
- clothing and fashion
- food and wine production
- chemicals/petrochemicals
- agriculture
- shipping
- tourism

Employment for foreigners

Executive and professional

Italy is a very good location for executive and professional jobs, both for postings and direct application. Many British companies have subsidiaries. Good career jobs are available and executive rates of pay are excellent. Suitably qualified people could approach employers in their particular sphere of interest.

Skilled and casual

British people can apply to take any job in Italy, but would need to speak good Italian to stand a reasonable chance of success. A notable number of British expatriates are employed in the food processing, textiles, fashion and electronics industries. There is a notable demand for English-speaking secretaries and PAs, teachers of English as a foreign language (who do not necessarily have to be qualified) and au pairs. Some casual work is available in tourism, mainly in the Italian Alps, Dolomites and Apennines (November-April).

Advice to job-hunters

The potential is much better in northern Italy than the south, which suffers from severe unemployment. Some employers are reluctant to employ foreigners due to the bureaucracy the Government imposes. So far as casual work goes there is much unofficial work, paid in cash. In the south the Mafia influence pervades much business.

Many industries are run by state controlled companies, like IRI, ENI and ENEL, but EU nationals are permitted to apply for these jobs.

Finding sources of work

Jobs can be found from the UK or in Italy. Qualified personnel stand a good chance through the OPU but they should speak Italian also. Otherwise try private UK agencies; executives should check with recruitment consultancies and also look at the possibility of a posting. Private employment agencies are not permitted in Italy.

The state employment service

The Italian state employment agency is the **Ufficio di Collocamento Mandopera**. It can be unhelpful to foreigners but will be of help to those who can speak some Italian. See the *Yellow Pages* for local offices, under the heading of 'Ufficio del Lavoro'.

Using newspapers

Italian newspapers are both a good source of vacancies and can be used to advertise Situations Wanted with some success. The main ones are *Il Messaggero*, *Corriere della Sera*, *La Repubblica*, *La Voce Repubblicana* (Rome), *La Nazione* (Florence), *Corriere della Sera* and *Il Giornale* (Milan), *La Stampa* (Turin), *Il Giornale di Napoli* (Naples), and *Il Gazzetino* (Venice). Executives should refer to Italian professional journals, details in *Benn's Media Directory International*.

Making direct applications

Contacts are very important in Italy and employers will often recruit on the spot to cover for busy times, especially in tourism or TEFL institutes. Working travellers should try door-knocking. Letters, however, should be in Italian. Addresses can be obtained from the local *Yellow Pages* or *Kompass* directory. Membership lists of companies to try are available from:

The British Chamber of Commerce
Via Camperio 9
Milan.
Tel: 02 877798 Web: www.infosquare.it/bcci

The Italian Chamber of Commerce for Great Britain
1 Princes Street
London W1R 8AY
Tel: (020) 7495 8191.

What are working conditions like?

Italy has complex employment legislation but there is a great tendency towards unofficial, black market working, especially in the south. As in some Latin countries some employers are less than scrupulous. Experience reveals that it is extremely difficult to obtain a contract of employment from all but the largest Italian firms. A degree of patience and persistence is essential in Italy, as the pace of business is very easy going in the more industrious north.

Minimum wage rates exist in Italy for most categories of work.

Living conditions

There is a great difference between north and south. The former has a very high standard of living akin to France, Germany or the UK, but the south is more like Greece or Spain. For more information, see *Living & Working in Italy*, written by Amanda Hinton and published by How To Books.

Working conditions in Italy

Average salary	Executive	£30,550
	Skilled worker	£18,400
Working week	40 hours	
Holiday entitlement	20 days, most expect 30	
Minimum fringe benefits	Extensive benefits such as housing and transport allowances, extra holiday entitlement and bonuses are expected by all but vary from company to company.	
Income tax rate	10-65 per cent	
Unemployment rate	11 per cent	
Trade unions	Very active but membership is voluntary.	

Living conditions in Italy

Living costs	Higher than UK, especially in north	
Average 3-bed house	To buy	£125,000
	To rent (month)	£400, outside cities
Social security system	Sickness, industrial accident, pensions and family allowances are generous. Hospital treatment is not free but most of the cost is covered by a state insurance scheme.	
Education	Reasonably good. Free to EU nationals.	
Standard of living	High in cities of the north but rural areas in south can be backward.	

Residence permits

EU nationals do not require work permits but must have a residence permit for stays longer than three months. If you intend to stay longer than three months apply within eight days of arrival to the nearest police station (Questura, Commissariato or Stazione di Carabinieri). They will issue you with a **Permit of Stay** called a **Carta di Soggiorno di Cittadino di Uno Stato Membro Della CEE**.

Embassies

Italian Embassy
14 Three Kings Yard
London W1Y 2EH.
Tel: (020) 7312 2200
Email: emblondon@embitaly.org.uk
Web: http://www.embitaly.org.uk

British Embassy
80 Via Venti Settembre
00100 Rome.
Tel: 06 482 5441.

There are British Consulates in Cagliari, Florence, Genoa, Milan, Naples, Trieste and Venice.

Major UK companies in Italy

Amstrad, Beecham, Castrol, Croda, EMI, ICI, Lucas, Prudential Assurance, Rover, Racal, Rowntree Mackintosh.

Language courses

Berlitz, 9–13 Grosvenor Street, London W1A 3BZ. Tel: (020) 7915 0909. In Rome: Tel: 06 654 0951.

Inlingua, 28 Rotton Park Road, Birmingham B16 9JL. Tel: (0121) 454 0204.

Linguaphone, Carlton Plaza, 111 Upper Richmond Road, London SW15 2TJ. Tel: (020) 8333 4900.

Universita per Stranieri di Siena, Via Pantaneto 45, 53100 Siena, Italy. Tel: +39 0577 240 111.

Centro di Lingua e Cultura Italiana per Stranieri, S. Spiritiop, 450124 Firenze, Italy. Tel: +39 0552 396 966 Fax: +39 055 280 800.

More useful contacts for Italy

The British-Italian Society, 21–22 Grosvenor Street, London W1X 9FE. Tel: (020) 7495 5536.

Italian Commercial & Technical Translations, 585a Fulham Road, London SW6 5UA. Tel: (020) 7381 0967.

The Italian Cultural Institute, 39 Belgrave Square, London SW1. Tel: (020) 7235 1461. Library, language courses and cultural facilities.

Italian State Tourist Office, 1 Princes Street, London W1. Tel: (020) 7408 1254.
Italian Translations, 86 The Ridings, London W5 3DR. Tel: (020) 8998 3024.
The Italian Trade Centre, 37 Sackville Street, London W1. Tel: (020) 7734 2412.
Italian Travel, 74 Cleveland Street, London W1. Tel: (020) 7430 0991.
Italy Visitors Club, 74 Cleveland Street, London W1. Tel: (020) 7636 8868.

LUXEMBOURG

What is the overall potential?

Luxembourg is the smallest country in Europe (population 400,000) and as a result does not hold great employment potential. However, the expatriate population is larger than in many other places of similar size, and is especially notable for the large proportion of executive and professional people.

Luxembourg is home to a large number of administrative offices — the Grand Duchy occupies a strategic economic position in that France, Germany and Belgium are all within easy reach. The European Parliament and Court of Justice of the EC are also based in Luxembourg.

Main industries

Luxembourg's main industries are service based and include banking and finance, telecommunications, insurance, tourism, broadcasting and transport. There are few primary and manufacturing industries but those in operation include agriculture, steel, plastics, chemicals and textiles.

About five per cent of the workforce, numbering 8,000 people, are employed in the EU institutions.

Employment for foreigners

It is difficult for foreigners to find unskilled work and casual jobs in Luxembourg. Such opportunities are mainly restricted to work in agriculture and the hotel and catering industry. Most expatriates in the Grand Duchy are of professional status. Those in banking and finance, insurance, chemicals and textiles are likely to have the widest range of opportunities; if appropriate, investigate the opportunities for a posting.

Advice to job-hunters

English is quite widely spoken in Luxembourg and there are a few executive jobs which will call for no language ability. However, many jobs call not only for fluency in English but fluency in French or German or both. It is largely unnecessary to speak the local language, Luxembourgeois.

Finding sources of work

All the main methods of finding work can be employed, but employment is mainly pre-arranged, rather than found on the spot. Several UK employment agencies are active and, as mostly executive jobs are involved, the CEPEC guide is a good source of these. Private agencies in Luxembourg can be located through the Luxembourg *Yellow Pages* (called *Ligne Bleue*).

Those with sought after qualifications should apply through the OPU. The Luxembourg national employment service is called **l'Administration de l'Emploi** and it is at 2 rue Claire Fontaine, 9201 Dierkerch, Luxembourg. Tel: +35 2 802 9291.

Using newspapers

The main newspapers are *Luxemburger Wort* and *Tageblatt*. Vacancies are also advertised in the main French and German newspapers, such as *Républican Lorrain*. Executives should see professional journals, including those published in the UK, France and Germany.

Making direct applications

Speculative applications are a good way of finding work for those with a particular skill to offer. Information on companies operating may be obtained from:

British Chamber of Commerce for Luxembourg, BP 2740, L-1027 Luxembourg. Tel: 352 4239391.

What are working conditions like?

Standards are high in Luxembourg and executives may be offered contracts on the best international terms. Industrial relations are excellent (major strikes are almost unknown) and the incidence of absenteeism is the lowest in Europe. Pay and conditions are fixed by collective bargaining, very much as in France.

Living conditions

The standard of living is very high; costs and facilities reflect the executive and professional population. Accommodation in the budget sector can be hard to find. Living costs exceed the surrounding countries but

Working conditions in Luxembourg

Average salary	Executive	£34,000
	Skilled worker	£20,500
Working week	40 hours	
Holiday entitlement	25 days	
Minimum fringe benefits	Very few, as all are taxed. Profit sharing schemes are becoming popular.	
Income tax rate	10-56 per cent	
Unemployment rate	2 per cent	
Trade unions	Membership is 66 per cent, but unions are not militant.	

Living conditions in Luxembourg

Living costs	Higher than UK	
Average 3-bed house	To buy	£110,000
	To rent (month)	£1,000
Social security system	Benefits include health care benefits, pensions, family allowances and unemployment pay. Unemployment pay is paid at 80 per cent of the average monthly salary for the first 182 days.	
Education	Free to EU nationals and of a high standard.	
Standard of living	High, similar to Belgium.	

are by no means the highest in Europe. There are many who commute cross-border to live in the less costly parts of France.

Residence permits

EU nationals do not require a work permit, but must have a residence permit (Carte d'Identité) to stay longer than three months. This can be obtained from the Administration Communale.

Embassies

Luxembourg Embassy
27 Wilton Crescent
London SW1X 8SD
Tel: (020) 7235 6961.

British Embassy
14 boulevard Roosevelt
L-2450 Luxembourg
Tel: 229864.

Other useful addresses

Luxair (Luxembourg Airlines), Terminal 2, Heathrow Airport, London. Tel: (020) 8745 4254.

Luxembourg National Trade and Tourist Office, 122 Regent Street, London W1R 5FE. Tel: (020) 7434 2800.

See also the section on Belgium above.

THE NETHERLANDS

What is the overall potential?

The Netherlands has always had reasonably good links with the UK. The country does not necessarily attract a lot of foreign workers overall, but it is probably one of the easier European countries in which to find a job. People are generally receptive towards foreigners (3.5 per cent of the population are not Dutch) and English is spoken by many.

Employers often prefer to recruit foreigners (especially if they will do dirty work or work for less than the prescribed rates of pay).

Main industries

Chief industries offering employment include:

- engineering
- textiles
- agriculture
- food and drink
- oil and gas exploration and refining
- shipping.

Growing industries include:

- electronics
- computing and telecommunications
- construction
- tourism
- services.

Employment for foreigners

Executive/professional

A small number of qualified people go to the Netherlands to take up executive and professional jobs. Many people are posted and there are many multinational companies and British companies with subsidiaries in the Netherlands. The UK is the largest foreign investor by far.

Skilled and casual

British people find that they can do most jobs in Holland, especially if they learn the language. Teachers and nurses are sometimes recruited from the UK. Amsterdam is a popular place for casual working and one of the easiest cities to find jobs. Jobs in hotels, catering, shops, factories and warehouses are available. Many foreigners are recruited to work in the massive agricultural and bulb growing industry, centred on Lisse and Hillegom, where jobs are plentiful (but dirty and not well paid).

Advice to job-hunters

Jobs can be found from the UK but are often very easily discovered on the spot. This is more practical in the Netherlands than most other countries, if carefully planned.

Finding sources of work

Qualified personnel stand a good chance through the OPU. Otherwise, try private UK agencies as many deal with the Netherlands. Private employment agencies (Uitzendbureaux or Uitzendburo) are numerous in the Netherlands (several hundred in Amsterdam) and are used to dealing with foreigners. See the local *Yellow Pages* (*Gouden Gids*) which are available in main UK libraries. One of the largest agencies is:

Manpower
Singel 250
1016AB Amsterdam.
Tel: 020 624 2745
Web: http://www.manpower.nl

The state employment service

The state employment agency is **Gewestelijk Arbeidsbureau**, which is usually helpful to foreigners but may not have a lot of jobs to offer.

The Royal Netherlands Embassy will supply a list of all the other offices on request.

Using newspapers

Dutch newspapers are a good source. The main ones are *De Telegraaf, De Volkskrant* and *Het Parool* (Amsterdam), *Haagsche Courant* (The Hague) and *Utrechts Nieuwsblad* (Utrecht). Executives should subscribe to a bulletin called *De Vacature* from:

PO Box 7
7200 AA Zutphen.
Tel: 575 594911
Fax: 575 519970

Making direct applications

Speculative applications can be made direct to employers. Addresses can be obtained from the *Gouden Gids* or *Kompass Directory*. The Royal Netherlands Embassy will send a useful list of contacts but cannot offer jobs or find work.

Work for young people

Young people seeking casual work during the summer can apply to:

The Central Bureau voor de Arbeidsvoorziening
PO Box 5814
2280 AA Rijswijk.
Tel: 70 313 0 911

What are working conditions like?

Netherlands law is generous towards the employee — often at the expense of the employer. Employment legislation is extensive (two months' notice must be given to employees) and a minimum wage is paid to all employees aged 23 or over. Partly as a result, unemployment is high and employers like to employ transient foreigners who will work without a contract.

Living conditions

The Netherlands offers a high standard of living and this is more similar to the UK than most European countries. Most people lead a fairly easy-going lifestyle but the rest of the country is more formal than

Working conditions in the Netherlands

Average salary	Executive	£30,000
	Skilled worker	£19,000
Working week	38 hours	
Holiday entitlement	14 days, most employees expect 21	
Minimum fringe benefits	Housing benefits, travel benefits and training allowances are widespread.	
Income tax rate	14-72 per cent	
Unemployment rate	9 per cent	
Trade unions	Few people belong to unions and membership is always voluntary.	

Living conditions in the Netherlands

Living costs	Slightly more than UK	
Average 3-bed house	To buy	£85,000
	To rent (month)	£600
Social security system	Deductions from wages are high but so are social benefits. Hospitals are not free and either state or private health insurance is essential.	
Education	Good. Free to EU nationals. British schools available.	
Standard of living	High in both cities and rural areas.	

Amsterdam. Most people speak a little English. It is as well to learn some Dutch but this can be done after arrival.

Residence permits

EU nationals do not require a work permit but should apply for a residence permit within eight days of arrival, at a main police station.

Embassies

Royal Netherlands Embassy
38 Hyde Park Gate
London SW7 5DP.
Tel: (020) 7584 5040

British Embassy
Lange Voorhout 10
The Hague
2514 ED.
Tel: 070 427 0427
Web: http://www.britain.nl

Major UK companies in The Netherlands

Barclays Bank, Beecham, BP, GEC, Glaxo, ICL, ICI, Lloyds Bank, Midland Bank, National Westminster Bank, Phillips, Plessey, Rover, Shell.

Language courses

Linguaphone, Carlton Plasa, 111 Upper Richmond Road, London SW15 2TJ. Tel: (020) 8333 4900 Fax: (020) 8333 4883.

Other useful contacts

Anglo-Netherlands Society, PO Box 68, Unilever House, London EC4P 4BQ. Tel: (020) 7353 5729.

British Council, Keizergracht 343, 1016 EH Amsterdam. Tel: 622 36 44.

Dutch Chamber of Commerce, 307 High Holborn, London WC1. Tel: (020) 7405 1358.

Dutch Commercial & Technical Translations, 585a Fulham Road, London SW5 5UA. Tel: (020) 7381 0967.

Dutch Translations, 64 Queen Street, London EC4. Tel: (020) 7248 8707.

Ministry of Social Affairs & Employment, Visseringsplan 26, 2288 ER Rijswijk.

Netherlands-British Chamber of Commerce, Javastraat 96, 2585 The Hague. Tel: +31 70 3287100. Publishes a directory, *Major Companies in the Netherlands*, indicating turnover, activities and number of employees.

Netherlands Board of Tourism, 18 Buckingham Gate, London SW1 6LB. Fax: (020) 7828 7941 Email: information@nbt.org.uk Web: http://www.goholland.co.uk

Useful periodicals

Intermediair. Weekly jobs periodical published by Uitgeverij Intermediair, Postbus 3434, 1001 AE Amsterdam. The same firm publishes an annual directory of job opportunities for graduates (*Intermediair Jaarboek*).

NORWAY

What is the overall potential?

Norway is one of the smaller European countries in both size and population, and thus does not offer a great deal of potential for employment.

Immigration regulations are strict, and indeed ban most foreign workers with the exception of those from EU countries with which Norway has a reciprocal agreement. (Norway is not currently a member of the EU.)

Main industries

- light manufacturing
- agriculture
- fisheries
- mining
- shipping
- forestry
- paper products
- oil and gas.

Tourism is of some importance.

Employment for foreigners

Suitably qualified people are able to work in all Norway's main industries. Though other Scandinavians are preferred, there are occasional skills shortages. Most expatriates (but then only a small number) tend to be employed in oil and gas, shipping and engineering professions. Nurses and teachers may also be recruited.

Casual

Many casual jobs are available (Norwegians are unwilling to do dirty or boring work) but it is hard to get work permits for these. Working travellers can sometimes find work on farms, in tourism and in factories or fishing. Au pairs are also accepted.

Advice to job-hunters

Employment should always be organised from the UK first, although speculative job-hunting visits are now allowed.

Finding sources of work

There are no UK agencies which specialise in Norway, but some of the agencies operating in the oil and gas industries may offer vacancies there. There are no private employment agencies in Norway.

The state employment service

The Norwegian state employment agency, called **Arbeidsdirektoratet**, may help foreigners direct. Their head office is at:

Holbergs Plass 7
Postboks 8127 Dep
Oslo 1
Tel: 02 11 10 70.

Using newspapers

Newspapers which can be used include *Dagbladet*, *Aftenposten* (Oslo) and the journal *Arbeiderbladet*.

Making direct applications

The best chance of finding work is by speculative methods, preferably by letter from the UK. Professional/executive level applicants should circulate their CV to all major companies with the chance of opening up a lead.

The Norwegian Chamber of Commerce
5 Lower Regent Street
London SW1Y 4LR
Tel: (020) 7930 0181

can pass on details of members.

Work for young people

Young working travellers can approach farms or hotels for casual work. However, it is better to apply through the **Working Guest Programme**, which can offer farm work to young people aged 18-30. The programme is run by:

Atlantis-Norwegian Foundation for Youth Exchange
Director International Programs
Rolf Hofmosgate 18
0655 Oslo 6.

What are working conditions like?

Working conditions in Norway

Average salary	Executive	£34,000
	Skilled worker	£23,000
Working week	40 hours maximum	
Holiday entitlement	28 days, plus 10 public holidays	
Minimum fringe benefits	Productivity bonuses possible, also paid training.	
Income tax rate	30-53 per cent	
Unemployment rate	2 per cent	
Trade unions	Works organisations are popular.	

Living conditions

Living conditions in Norway

Living costs	Much higher than UK	
Average 3-bed house	To buy	£140,000
	To rent (month)	£1,350
Social security system	State benefits paid are generous but social security deductions from wages high. There is a reciprocal agreement for hospital treatment between the UK and Norway.	
Education	Good	
Standard of living	Very high, but wages not as high as other high-cost countries.	

Entry regulations

EU citizens do not require work permits. However, a residence permit is required. This should be obtained from the local police as soon as you find employment or within three months of entry at the latest. You may be asked to leave Norway after three months if you do not have either employment or adequate means of financial support.

Embassies

Royal Norwegian Embassy
25 Belgrave Square
London SW1X 8QD.
Tel: (020) 7591 5500
Email: morten@embassy.norway.org.uk
Web: http://www.norway.org.uk

British Embassy
Thomas Heftyesgate 8
0244 Oslo 2.
Tel: 23 13 27 00
Email: britemb@online.no
Web: http://www.home.sol.no/britemb/

Major UK companies in Norway

BP, British Steel, Castrol, ICI, ICL, Reckitt & Colman, Smith & Nephew, Thorn EMI.

Language courses

Linguaphone, Carlton Plasa, 111 Upper Richmond Road, London SW15 2TJ. Tel: (020) 8333 4900 Fax: (020) 8333 4883

Six-week summer courses are held at the University of Oslo in Norwegian language and culture. For full information write to University of Oslo, International Office, Administration Building, 2 Floor, PO Box 1081, Blindern, Oslo. Tel: 22 85 84 50 Fax: 22 85 84 88 Email: international@admin.uio.no. The University also runs an International Summer School. This includes, in English, general courses on Norway and Norwegian language, plus postgraduate courses in subjects such as education, urban planning, and health services. Scholarships are available for those wishing to attend. Full details of each year's programme can be obtained from International Summer School, University of Oslo, PO Box 13, Blindern, N-0313 Oslo. Tel: 22 85 63 85 Fax: 22 85 41 99 Email: iss@admin.uio.no

Three-week intensive summer courses are run by the University of Bergen. Some scholarships may be available.

Useful periodical

Dagbladet, the leading newspaper.

Other useful contacts

Anglo-Norse Society, 25 Belgrave Square, London SW1X 8QD. Tel: (020)7591 5500 Fax: (020) 7245 6993.

Norwegian Club, Charles House, Regent Street, London SW1Y 4LR. Tel: (020) 7839 6242.

Norwegian Commercial & Technical Translations, 585a Fulham Road, London SW6 5UA. Tel: (020) 7381 0967.

Norwegian Ministry of Foreign Affairs, Press and Cultural Relations, PO Box 8114, Oslo 1 Tel: 22 24 36 00 Fax: 22 24 95 00 (information service for foreign students).

Norwegian School in London, 28 Arteberry Road, London SW20 8AH. Tel: (020) 8947 6627.

Norwegian Tourist Board, Charles House, 5 Lower Regent Street, London SW1. Tel: (020) 7839 6255.

Norwegian YWCA, 52 Holland Park, London SW11. Tel: (020) 7727 9897.

PORTUGAL

What is the overall potential?

Portugal is one of the EU's least industrialised countries and, subsequently, one of the poorer states. It has not developed like Spain, neither does it share the massive tourist income of both Spain and Greece. Most expatriates work here for the fine weather and relaxed pace of life, rather than career opportunities. British people tend to be well received.

Main industries

Portugal is still largely an agricultural country, and labour-intensive agriculture and fisheries are mainstays. Large industries include:

- textiles
- clothing
- footwear
- food processing
- tourism (in the south).

Smaller industries include:

- steel
- shipbuilding/repair
- minerals
- light engineering
- motor manufacture.

Employment for foreigners

Executive and professional
Currently, few executive/professional people are recruited directly by Portuguese industry. Many people working here are posted, several British companies have branches or subsidiaries. Most industries are difficult to penetrate unless fluent Portuguese is spoken.

Casual
Casual work can be taken. Principal areas are:

- tourism
- au pair/nannying
- English teaching

but pay can be low.

Advice to job-hunters

Executives should confine their search to Lisbon which is the only large industrial and commercial city. Tourism is confined largely to Lisbon and Estoril, and the Algarve in the south. It is seasonal, summer only. For a good practical introduction to Portugal see *Living & Working in Portugal* by Sue Tyson-Ward (How To Books 1993).

Finding sources of work

Jobs are best found in advance if possible, due to their small numbers. It can be easier to find vacancies on the spot but success rate will be low. Few private UK agencies deal with Portugal. Private employment agencies (mainly in Lisbon) could be tried; see details in Portuguese *Yellow Pages*.

The state employment service
The state employment agency is not used to helping foreigners, but the determined could approach:

Ministério do Trabalho e da Solidariedade
Praça de Londres
1091 Lisbon Codex.
Tel: (21) 844 11 00

Using newspapers

Newspapers are a good source of vacancies or can be used to advertise. The main ones are *Correio da Manha*, *O Diario*, *Diario de Noticias*, *Jornal de O Dia* (Lisbon) and *Jornal de Noticias* (Oporto). There are now several English language newspapers in Portugal. Some are published by:

Universal Media Ltd
75a Marylebone High Street
London W1M 3AR.
Tel: (020) 7935 9134

These include *Portugal Post* and *Algarve News*. There is also the *Anglo-Portuguese News*, good for casual vacancies.

Making direct applications

Speculative applications can be made direct to employers. Obtain addresses from the *Yellow Pages* at UK libraries, or the *Kompass* directories. Employers, especially in tourism and the English teaching institutes, will recruit on the spot to cover busy periods.

The Portuguese Embassy/Consulate will not help.

The Hispanic & Luso Brazilian Council, Canning House, 2 Belgrave Place, London SW1X 8PJ Tel: (020) 7235 2303 Fax: (020) 7235 3587 have two leaflets available: *Portugal, a Guide to Employment Opportunities for Young People*, and *Portuguese Courses in Portugal.* Price £3 each.

The British-Portuguese Chamber of Commerce
Rua da Estrela 8
Lisbon.
Tel: (21) 390 44 00 Fax: (21) 390 15 13

and

British Embassy
33 Rua de São Bernardo
1249-082 Lisbon.

may offer unofficial advice and contacts.

Work for young people

Young people seeking holiday jobs and cultural exchanges should approach:

The Instituto Português da Juventude
Avenida da Liberdade 194
1200 Lisbon.
Tel: 01 352 2694
Email: juventude@mail.telepac.pt
Web: www.sejuventude.pt

What are working conditions like?

Portugal currently offers much lower wages than the UK and taxes can be high for above average earners. Portugal has extensive labour legislation, and equal rights for women at work, which is much more progressive than many other more modern European countries. Business can be informal and hours worked on an as-needed basis.

Working conditions in Portugal

Average salary	Executive	£21,000
	Skilled worker	£11,500
Working week	38 hours, but flexible	
Holiday entitlement	28 days and many public holidays	
Minimum fringe benefits	13th month bonus. Some receive 14th month bonus. Social security contributions paid for the lower paid.	
Income tax rate	4-60 per cent, average 35 per cent	
Unemployment rate	18 per cent	
Trade unions	Active in some places but foreigners do not usually join.	

Living conditions

Portugal offers a pleasant, relaxed way of life. Living costs and property prices or rents are still low and daily living costs still amazingly cheap outside tourist centres. Facilities for expatriates are good in Lisbon and the Algarve but other areas can be very remote.

Living conditions in Portugal

Living costs	Lower than UK.
Average 3-bed house	To buy £35,000, outside resorts To rent (month) £320 (£600 in Lisbon)
Social security system	Contributions are deducted from wages by the Caixa de Previdência. The state pays all but a small part of medical expenses.
Education	Standards vary but there are International Schools in Lisbon and the Algarve.
Standard of living	Modest, even in towns.

Residence permits

EU nationals do not need work permits. However, a residence permit, known as a **Residência**, is required for stays exceeding 60 days. This can be obtained at an office of the **Serviço de Estrangeiros** (Alien Registration Office).

Embassies

Portuguese Embassy
11 Belgrave Square
London SW1X 8PP.
Tel: (020) 7235 5331
Email: Portembassy-london@dialin.net
Web: http://www.portembassy.gla.ac.uk

British Embassy
33 Rua de São Bernardo
1249-082 Lisbon.
Tel: 01 392 4000
Fax: 01 392 4185
Web: http://www.uk-embassy.pt

Major UK companies in Portugal

Barclays Bank, BP, Commercial Union, Glaxo, Hoover, ICI, ICL, Metal Box, Prudential Insurance, Rank Xerox, Rover, Shell.

Language courses

Linguaphone, Carlton Plaza, 111 Upper Richmond Road, London SW15 2TJ. Tel: (020) 8333 4900 Fax: (020) 8333 4883.

Inlingua, 28 Rotton Park Road, Birmingham B16 9JL. Tel: (0121) 454 0204.

Inlingua, Rua Sa Bandeira, Oporto. Tel: (22) 339 44 00.

Portuguese Language School,70 Upper Richmond Road, London SW15 2RP. Tel: (020) 8877 1738.

Other useful contacts

The News, Urbanizaçao Lagoa Sol Lt 3–r/c–D–Lagoa 8400 Lagoa Tel: (82) 341 200.

Anglo-Portuguese Society, 2 Belgrave Square, London SW1X 8PJ. Tel: (020) 7245 9738.

British Council, Rua de Sâo Marçal 174, 1294 Lisbon Codex. Tel: (21) 347 6141 Fax: (21) 343 0015.

Portugala Holidays Ltd, 94 Fortis Green, London N2 9EY. Tel: (020) 8444 1857.

Portuguese National Tourist Office, 22–25a Sackville Street, London W1X 1DE. Tel: (020) 7494 1441.

Portuguese Translations, 64 Queen Street, London EC4. Tel: (020) 7248 8707.

Portuguese Travel, 13 Beauchamp Place, London SW3. Tel: (020) 7581 3104.

SPAIN

What is the overall potential?

Over the last few years Spain has been making the transition from an economy based on agriculture and tourism to that of a mainstream western European economy. Many European companies have invested in Spain as a cost-effective manufacturing base and this is expected to continue. The service sector is also growing fast.

Having said all this many expatriates in Spain have retired there; only about five per cent of the British population of 230,000 are employed.

Main industries

Spain was traditionally an agricultural economy and this is still important. The tourist industry is a major revenue earner, though growth has levelled of late. Mining and mineral exploitation and steel production are important older industries. Modern industries include:

- motor manufacture
- shipbuilding
- clothing and textiles
- chemicals
- light engineering.

Employment for foreigners

Executive and professional

In the past few years executive/professional people have not found a great deal of demand for their services. But in many cases — such as the chemical, engineering and motor industries — Spain is now actively recruiting on a Europe-wide level.

Unskilled and casual

Spain should offer good potential for unskilled workers and casual staff who want to work in the sun; many Spanish industries are expanding. Traditional areas for recruitment of Britons are in:

- teaching English as a foreign language (TEFL), for which it is not always necessary to be experienced or qualified
- and tourism: guides, couriers, entertainers, etc.

Many casual jobs should be available in the holiday resorts, depending on demand at the time. Au pairs and nannies can also find openings.

Advice to job-hunters

Spain is a large country but 70 per cent of all executive vacancies are in Madrid or Barcelona. Casual job-seekers are best advised to keep to the resorts and islands patronised by British holidaymakers. Other parts of Spain can be remarkably untouched by the business and tourist booms and have few openings for foreigners, together with high unemployment.

Finding sources of work

Jobs can be found from the UK, but it may be better to apply on the spot in Spain. Few UK employment agencies deal with Spain. Executives who speak Spanish could canvass the recruitment consultancies which operate in Madrid.

The state employment service

The Spanish state employment agency cannot offer much help unless enquiries are directed in Spanish. Preliminary enquiries can be directed to:

INEM (Instituto Nacional de Empleo)
Calle Condesa de Venadito, 9
Madrid 28027.
Tel: (91) 585 98 88
Fax: (91) 377 58 87

Using newspapers

Spanish newspapers are probably the best source of vacancies and can also be used to advertise Situations Wanted. The main ones are *El Pais* and *Diario 16* (Madrid), *La Vanguardia* and *Diari de Barcelona* (Barcelona), *El Diario de la Costa del Sol* (Malaga) and *El Correo de Andalucia* (Seville). There are also several English language newspapers in the tourist areas, published by:

Universal Media Ltd
75a Marylebone High Street
London W1M 3AR.
Tel: (020) 7935 9134

They include *Sur in English*, *Costa Blanca News* and the *Iberian Daily Sun*.

Making direct applications

Speculative applications can be made direct to employers. Obtain addresses from *Yellow Pages (Paginas Amarillas)* at some UK libraries, or refer to British package holiday companies direct. Also try the *Kompass* directory. It is often better to call on potential employers rather than write, as bosses often do not plan ahead and will recruit on the spot at busy times.

The Spanish Embassy/Consulate will not help.

The Hispanic & Luso Brazilian Council, Canning House, 2 Belgrave Place, London SW1X 8PJ Tel: (020) 7235 2303 Fax: (020) 7235 3587 have two leaflets available: *Spain, a Guide to Employment Opportunities for Young People*, and *Spanish Courses in Spain*.

The British Chamber of Commerce
Marques de Valdeiglas 3

Madrid.
Tel: (+34) 915383500
can supply a list of members.

Work for young people
Young people seeking au pair vacancies and working exchanges may contact:
Club de Relaciones Culturales Internacionales
Calle de Feraz 28
Madrid 28008.
Tel: (91) 541 71 03

What are working conditions like?

Spain currently has some of the lowest wages in the EU, and taxation is no longer as low as it used to be. Employees are entitled to prescribed minimum rates of pay, security of employment and, for the lower paid, social security contributions paid by the employer. Rights are, however, not always readily granted and are difficult to enforce through the courts.

Working conditions in Spain

Average salary	Executive	£23,500
	Skilled worker	£14,000
Working week	40 hours, but varies	
Holiday entitlement	21 days; there are many local public holidays	
Minimum fringe benefits	13th and 14th month bonuses in July and December	
Income tax rate	8-56 per cent	
Unemployment rate	up to 19 per cent	
Trade unions	Active in some industries. Foreigners rarely participate.	

Living conditions

Spain attracts people largely due to its good weather and relaxed standard of living, even in Madrid or Barcelona. Property prices and living costs are some of the lowest in Europe but may soon equal France or the UK. There are considerable variations between the holiday resorts and large cities, which can be remarkably prosperous and modern, and areas of the interior which may still have a very basic way of life.

Living conditions in Spain

Living costs	Daily costs lower than UK
Average 3-bed house	To buy £40,000, outside resorts To rent (month) £400, outside resorts
Social security system	Social security benefits and hospital treatment are not free. Most employees can decide whether to take private insurance schemes or join the state scheme run by Instituto Nacional de Previsión.
Education	Free to EU nationals. English education available (fee paying) in many places.
Standard of living	Good in cities/towns but rural areas can be surprisingly backward.

Residence permits

EU nationals do not need work permits. However, a residence permit *is* required and this can be obtained at a main police station. EU nationals may stay for three months without a permit, but it is advisable to apply soon after arrival. Initially you may be issued with a **Permanencia** and then a **Residencia**.

Embassies

Spanish Embassy
39 Chesham Place
London SW1X 8SB.
Tel: (020) 7235 5555

British Embassy
Calle de Fernando el Santo 16
Madrid 4.
Tel: 91 319 0200

Major UK companies in Spain

BP, British Steel, Brooke Bond Oxo, Cadbury Schweppes, Commercial Union, Fisons, ICI, Midland Bank, Plessey, Royal Insurance, Thomson, Wimpey.

Language courses

Berlitz, 9–13 Grosvenor Street, London W1A 3BZ. Tel: (020) 7915 0909. In Madrid: Tel: 01 541 6103.

Linguaphone, Carlton Plasa, 111 Upper Richmond Road, London SW15 2TJ. Tel: (020) 8333 4900 Fax: (020) 8333 4883.

Inlingua, 28 Rotton Park Road, Birmingham B16 9JL. Tel: (0121) 454 0204.

Instituto Cervantes, 102 Eaton Square, London SW1W 9AN. Tel: (020) 7235 0353 Fax: (020) 7235 0329.

Translation services

Spanish Commercial and Technical Translations, 585a Fulham Road, London SW6 5UA. Tel: (020) 7381 0967.

Spanish Language Services, 12 Bridge Wharf, 156 Caledonian Road, London N1. Tel: (020) 7713 8013 Fax: (020) 7713 8014. Email: SpanishLS@cs.com

Spanish Technical Translations, 73 Queens Gate, London SW7. Tel: (020) 7244 8906.

Spanish Translation Service, 107a St Paul's Road, Islington, London N1 2NA. Tel: (020) 7359 9634 Fax: (020) 7704 6274.

Spanish Translations, 64 Queens St, London EC4. Tel: (020) 7248 8707.

Periodicals

Costa Golf, Apartado 358, Loma de los Riscos 1, Torremolinos 29620 (Málaga). Tel: (95) 238 1542. Monthly.

Sur in English, Avenida Dr Maranon 48, E29009 Malaga. Tel: 95 264 96 00 Fax: 95 261 12 56 Email: sureng@surinenglish.com Web: http://www.surinenglish.com

More useful contacts

British Consulates in Spain

The British Consulate, Edificio Cataluña PO Box 2020, 5 Luis Morote 6-3, Puerto de la Luz, 35007 Las Palmas, Canary Islands. Tel: 26 25 08 Fax: 26 77 74.

The British Consulate, Plaza Nueva 8-Dpdo, 41001 Seville. Tel: 422 88 75 Fax: 421 03 23.

The British Consulate-General, Avda Diagonal 477-13°, 08036 Barcelona. Tel: 419 9044 Fax: 405 2411 Email: brconbcn@alba.mssl.es

The British Consulate-General, Alameda Urquizo 2-8, 48008 Bilbao. Tel: 415 76 00 Fax: 416 76 32.

The British Consulate-General, Plaza Calvo Sotelo 172-1, Apartado 564, Alicante. Tel: (96) 521 60 22.

The British Consulate-General, Avda Isidoro Macabich 45-1, Apartado 307, Ibiza. Tel: (97) 130 18 18.

The British Consulate-General, Edificio Duquesa, Duquesa de Parcent 4-1, Málaga. Tel: (95) 221 75 71.

The British Consulate-General, Plaza Mayor 3D, Palma de Mallorca 12. Tel: (97) 171 24 45.

The British Consulate-General, Paseo de Pereda 27, Santander. Tel: (94) 222 00 00.

The British Consulate-General, Plaza Weyler 8-1, Santa Cruz de Tenerife. Tel: (922) 2868 63.

The British Consulate-General, Plaza Compostela 23-6, Apartado 49, Vigo. Tel: (98) 43 71 33.

Spanish Consulates in Britain

The Spanish Consulate, 70 Spring Gardens, Manchester M2 2BQ.

The Spanish Consulate-General, 20 Draycott Place SW3. Tel: (020) 7589 8989. Residence visas. Tel: (020) 7581 5924. Tourist visas. Tel: (020) 7581 5925. Notary. Tel: (020) 7225 0003. Registro Civil (day). Tel: (020) 7584143. Emergencies (out of hours). Tel: (020) 7584 5143.

Travel contacts in Britain

Instituto Cervantes, 102 Eaton Square SW1W 9AN. Tel: (020) 7235 0353 Fax: (020) 7235 0329.

Spanish Airlines (IBERIA), Venture House, 29 Glass House St, London W1R 6JU. Tel: (020) 7830 0011.

Spanish Aviation Services, 57B Lupus Street SW1. Tel: (020) 7821 5801.

Spanish National Tourist Office, 22–23 Manchester Square, London W1M 5AP.

Trásmediterraneo, Melia Travel, 12 Dover St, London W1. Tel: (020) 7409 1884.

Travel contacts in Spain

Ayuntamientos (Town Halls)

Central de Reservas e Información Internacional, Instituto de la Juventud, calle José Ortega y Gasset 71, 28006 Madrid. Tel: (091) 401 95 01 (Youth Hostels).

Consejeros de Turismo (Ministers of Tourism, one in each region).

Iberrail SA, calle Capitán Haya 55, 28020 Madrid.Tel: (91) 571 5972.

Información RENFE (Spanish Railways), Tel: (902) 24 02 02. International Enquiries (93) 490 11 22.

Ministerio de Cultura, Instituto de la Juventud, José Ortega y Gasset 71, 28006 Madrid. Tel: (91) 401 95 01 (youth or student travel).

Real Automóvil Club de España (RACE), José Abascal 10, 28003 Madrid. Tel: (91) 447 33 59. The equivalent of the AA.

TIVE, Fernando el Católico 88, 28015 Madrid. Tel: (91) 543 0208 (student travel).

Turespana (Tourist Offices), calle Duque de Medinaceli 2, Madrid. Tel: (91) 429 4951 Fax: (91) 429 09 09.

Accommodation

Cubits Spanish Properties, 26 York Street, London W1H. Tel: (020) 7935 7970.

Keytel International, 402 Edgware Road, London W2 1ED. Tel: (020) 7616 0300.

Melia Hotels, calle Orense 81, 28020 Madrid. Tels: (91) 571 50 40, 571 16 16.

Novotel, calle Albacete 1, 28037 Madrid. Tel: (91) 326 75 42 Fax: (91) 404 11 05.

Santos Hoteles, calle Juan Bravo 8, Madrid. Tels: (91) 431 21 37, 431 18 97.

Business contacts in Britain

Department of Trade and Industry Overseas Trade Division (Spain Desk), 1 Victoria St, London SW1H 0ET. Tels: (020) 7215 4284 (capital goods), 215 5624 (consumer goods) Fax: (020) 7215 4711.

The Spanish Embassy (Commercial Office), 66 Chiltern Street, London W1M 2LS. Tel: (020) 7486 0101.

Business contacts in Spain

Barclays Bank, Madrid Main Branch, Plaza de Col¢n 1, 28046 Madrid. Tel: (91) 336 1000.

British Council, Paseo del General Martínez, Campos 31, 28010 Madrid. Tel: (91) 337 3500 Fax: (91) 337 3573 Email: general.enquiries@es.britcoun.org

FAB—Foreign Advice Bureau, calle Cruz 5, Torremolinos, 29620 Málaga. Tels: (952) 383022, 383653, 388736.

General Directorate of Foreign Commerce, Paseo de la Castellana 14–16, 28046 Madrid. Tel: (91) 349 61 00 Fax: (91) 431 61 28.

The Legal Department, Spanish Embassy, 39 Chesham Place, London SW1X 8SB. (Background information on buying property in

Spain, Spanish succession law and setting up business in Spain.)

Lloyds Bank International plc, calle Serrano 90, 28006 Madrid. Postal address: Apartado Postal 64, 28080 Madrid. Tel: (91) 409 73 48.

Ministry of Agriculture (Ministerio de Agricultura, Pescay Alimentación), Paseo Infanta Isabel 1, 28014 Madrid. Tel: (91) 347 56 00 Fax: (91) 467 58 54.

Ministry of Economy and Finance (Ministerio de Economía y Hacienda), calle Alcalá 9, 28014, Madrid. Tel: (91) 595 80 00 Fax: (91) 595 88 37.

Ministry of External Affairs (Ministerio de Asuntas Exteriores), Plaza de la Provincia 1, 28012 Madrid. Tel: (91) 364 26 47 Fax: (91) 266 70 76.

Ministry of Industry and Energy (Ministerio Industria y Energía), Paseo de la Castellana 160, 28071 Madrid. Tel: (91) 349 49 76 Fax: (91) 457 80 66.

Ministry of Labour and Social Security (Ministerio de Trabajo y Asuntos Sociales), calle Bretón de los Herreros 41, 28003 Madrid. Tel: (91) 441 15 00 Fax: (91) 399 25 44.

Further reading on Spain

Blackstone Franks Guide to Living in Spain (Beekman PubInc 1989). 208pp, with map.

Busselle, Michael, *Discovering Spain* (Pavilion Books 1999).

Credades, Bernado M. (ed), *Spanish Business Law* (Kluwer Law International 1985). 656 pp.

Hopkins, A. & G. MacPherdran, *Explorer Spain* (AA Publishing 1999).

Hughes, Robert, *Barcelona* (Harvill Press 1999).

Monreal, Luis, *Castles of Spain* (Konemann UK Ltd., 1999).

Reay-Smith, John, *Living in Spain* (Hale 1995). 207pp, illustrated, with maps, and 16 plates.

Richards, Robert A. C., *Living & Working in Spain* (How To Books 1998). A practical handbook written by a long-term resident of Madrid.

Searl, David, *The Spanish Property Guide* (Santana Books 1998).

Walden, Hilaire, *The Book of Tapas and Spanish Cooking* (Salamander Books 1998).

SWEDEN

What is the overall potential?

At present, few expatriates work in Sweden. However, it is a prosperous country and does have some demand for workers from abroad. As with other countries the jobs tend to be either for the skilled and qualified or, at the other end of the spectrum, for casual workers to do dirty and boring jobs.

Main industries

Main industries are:

- mining
- minerals
- iron/steel
- engineering
- motor manufacture
- machinery
- chemicals
- timber
- paper.

Employment for foreigners

The majority of people from abroad are at management or director level in business and many of these are posted rather than appointed directly. The particular activities to which foreigners are recruited tend to be the mining, minerals, chemicals and engineering type industries. Sweden is a hard country to find casual work in; a small number of foreigners work in hotels and catering establishments in Stockholm and Gothenburg, or on farms. Doctors, nurses and teachers (especially English teachers) can sometimes be placed if they speak or learn some Swedish.

Advice to job-hunters

It is advisable to organise employment before arriving in Sweden, although speculative job-hunting trips are now allowed.

Finding sources of work

There are no private agencies in Sweden and no UK agencies deal with Sweden on a regular basis.

The state employment service

The state agency, called **Arbetsmarknadsstyrelsen**, may give general advice:

Kungstensgatan 45
113 99 Stockholm.
Tel: (08) 5860 6000
Fax: (08) 5860 6499
Email: arbetsmarknadsstyrelsen@ams.amv.se

Using newspapers

The best source of vacancies is Swedish newspapers. The main ones are *Svenska Dagbladet*, *Dagen*, *Expressen* and *Dagens Nyheter* (Stockholm) and *Göteborg Posten* (Gothenburg).

Making direct applications

Speculative applications can be made direct to employers. Executives should refer to trade directories such as *Kompass* for addresses.

The British Swedish Chamber of Commerce
Box 5501
S-11485 Stockholm.
Tel: (08) 7838 200
Fax: (08) 6650 935
Email: kerstin@bscc.ihb.se

can supply a list of businesses with British links. Casual workers should avoid travelling to Sweden, but make enquiries to hotels, etc by letter if possible.

Entry regulations

EU citizens do not require work permits. However, a residence permit is required. This should be obtained from the local police within three months of entry at the latest and will last for the period for which your job lasts, up to five years maximum. If you do not have employment you must have adequate financial means to support yourself.

Embassies

Swedish Embassy
11 Montagu Place
London W1H 2AL.
Tel: (020) 7917 6400
Email: embassy@swednet.org.uk
Web: http://www.swedish-embassy.org.uk/embassy/index.html

Working conditions in Sweden

Average salary	Executive	£38,000
	Skilled worker	£23,000
Working week	40 hours	
Holiday entitlement	35 days plus 12 public holidays	
Minimum fringe benefits	Social security contributions, bonuses, housing and travel allowances, health and welfare facilities and holiday allowances are all usual.	
Income tax rate	30-70 per cent approximately	
Unemployment rate	1 per cent	
Trade unions	Works organisations are popular and employee/employer relations are extremely good.	

Living conditions in Sweden

Living costs	Much higher than UK	
Average 3-bed house	To buy	£170,000
	To rent (month)	£1,000
Social security system	State benefits are very high. Hospital treatment is largely free to resident foreigners and British visitors.	
Education	Good	
Standard of living	Very high, especially in the south.	

British Embassy
Skarpögatan 6-8
11527 Stockholm.
Tel: (08) 667 0140

Major UK companies in Sweden

Barclays Bank, BOC, BP, British Steel, BTR, Castrol, EMI, GEC, Fisons, GKN, Glaxo, ICL, Lucas, Lever Brothers, Pilkington Glass.

Language courses

Linguaphone, Carlton Plaza, 111 Upper Richmond Road, London SW15 2TJ. Tel: (020) 8333 4900 Fax: (020) 8333 4883. Swedish language summer schools: courses last between two and ten weeks and are run by a number of organisations including:

Uppsala University International Summer Session, Box 513, S-751 20 Uppsala. Tel (010 4618) 12 08 29.

Details of dates, fees etc are contained in a booklet entitled *Svenska Institutets Internationalla Sommarkurser*, available from the Swedish Embassy from January or February each year, or write direct to the addresses given above.

Other useful contacts

Anglo-Swedish Society, 43 Kinburn Street, London SE16 1DN. Tel/Fax: (020) 7231 3664.

Kern Translations and Interpreting, 53–54 Chancery Lane, London WC2A 1QU. Tel: (020) 7831 5600 Fax: (020) 7831 5606 Email: kernuk@enterprise.net

Swedish Business Services Ltd, 91 Regent Street, London W1. Tel: (020) 7437 6259.

Swedish Chamber of Commerce, 72 Welbeck Street, London W1. Tel: (020) 7486 4545.585a Fulham Road, London SW6 5UA. Tel: (020) 7381 0967.

Swedish Commercial and Technical Translations, 585a Fulham Road, London SW6 5UA. Tel: (020) 7381 0967.

Swedish National Tourist Office, 3 Cork Street, London W1X 1HA. Tel: (020) 7724 5868.

Swedish Trade Council, 73 Welbeck Street, London W1. Tel: (020) 7935 9601.

SWITZERLAND

What is the general potential?

Switzerland is one of the most prosperous countries in the world and should offer good potential for expatriates both at executive level and for casual work. Indeed, Swiss employers are keen to employ foreigners. However, the fact that Switzerland is not an EU member makes it very difficult to take up the available jobs.

Main industries

Swiss industry focuses on high technology manufacturing and services. Main activities include:

- banking
- finance
- insurance
- chemicals
- pharmaceuticals
- textiles
- light engineering
- precision instruments (including watches)
- some electronic manufacturing
- food processing.

Agriculture is extensive and there is a large tourist industry, more important in winter.

Employment for foreigners

Executive and professional

Switzerland offers opportunities in all its main industries to those who are well qualified and experienced in their field. There is a shortage of some technical and scientific personnel. Many of the available jobs are filled by posting. However, Swiss employers are always willing and can afford to employ specialists and so speculative application can work at executive level. Nurses can also sometimes find posts.

Casual

Because most Swiss are well qualified and educated there is a shortage of staff to do most ordinary jobs, especially any work which is dirty and boring. This type of work is ideal for the working traveller, subject to being able to obtain a work permit, and the pay for this type of work is generous by UK standards. Most casual workers work in shops, hotels, bars, restaurants and tourist facilities throughout Switzerland, especially in the winter season (November-April).

Advice to job-hunters

It is advisable to locate a job before leaving the UK if at all possible. It is not legal to enter Switzerland to take up a job without a work permit (see later), although this does happen. Those who speak at least two of the Swiss languages of French, German and Italian, one fluently and the basics of another, stand a much better chance of finding a job.

Finding sources of work

State employment agencies, either in Switzerland or the UK, cannot help. There are some private employment agencies in both countries which can help executives and the professionally qualified. The following may have placements:

Eurecruit Ltd
27 Holywell Row
London EC2A 4JB.
Tel: (020) 7247 1407
Email: cv@eurecruit.demon.co.uk
Web: www.eurecruit.demon.co.uk

Europa IT Consultants
Brassey House
New Zealand Avenue
Walton on Thames.
Tel: (01932) 252795

Eurotech Employment Services
Canal Yard
Hayes Road
Southall.
Tel: (020) 8574 4560

Others can be located in the *Yellow Pages* for the relevant Swiss town.

Using newspapers

Swiss newspapers are a good source of vacancies and can also be used to advertise for work. The main ones are *Neue Zurcher Zeitung* (Zurich), *Basler-Zeitung* and *Baslerstab* (Basle), *Berner Zeitung* and *Berner Tagwacht* (Berne), *La Suisse*, *La Tribune de Geneve* and *Journal de Geneve* (Geneva).

Executive and professional work

Executives should refer to Swiss professional journals, also those in France and Germany, for Swiss vacancies. There is also an executive vacancy bulletin:

Le Journal de l'Emploi
rue de l'Araquebuse 8
1204 Geneva
Case postale 5411 1211.
Tel: 022 807 06 70
Fax: 022 807 06 89

Executives and professionals should circulate their details to all Swiss companies in their field; use *Yellow Pages* or *Kompass* directory as a guide. Lists of members who could be approached are available from:

The British-Swiss Chamber of Commerce
Freistrasse 155
CH 8032 Zurich.
Tel: 01 422 31 31
Fax: 01 422 32 44

Work for young people
Young people seeking casual work should canvass potential employers by letter or by personal calling. Hotels, bars and restaurants in tourist areas have many vacancies. Tourist offices may supply lists.

What are working conditions like?

The Swiss work very hard and the pace of business can be frantic, both for executives and casual workers. Working conditions are usually excellent and contracts secure. Switzerland is a high wage, high cost country. Even a hotel cleaner may earn £1,000+ per month in many places.

Working conditions in Switzerland

Average salary	Executive	£64,000
	Skilled worker	£33,000
Working week	38 hours	
Holiday entitlement	28 days	
Minimum fringe benefits	Productivity bonuses are becoming popular. Health insurance, school fees, sports club fees and cars are all costly and so may be offered as benefits.	
Income tax rate	12-33 per cent	
Unemployment rate	0.5 per cent	
Trade unions	Works organisations are popular.	

Living conditions

Switzerland is a clean, green country with a very high standard of living. However, it is a high cost country and it is advisable to plan your budget with care before leaving. For example, butter is £1.90 per half pound, meat approximately £9 per pound.

Living conditions in Switzerland

Living costs	Much higher than UK	
Average 3-bed house	To buy	£170,000+ (purchase is restricted for non-Swiss nationals)
	To rent (month)	£ 1,500+
Social security system	State benefits paid are limited. Most people join contributory insurance schemes to pay for hospital treatment and provide sick pay and pensions.	
Education	Good. There are several International Schools and British Schools.	
Standard of living	Very high.	

Entry regulations

As Switzerland is not currently an EU member a combined work and residence permit is required to live there. Applicants must first find an employer who has been authorised to employ foreigners. This employer will then supply the employee with an official document called an 'Assurance of a Residence Permit'. This must be presented when you enter Switzerland followed by registration with the Aliens Police within eight days.

The Assurance of a Residence Permit must be posted to the employee's address outside Switzerland and may not be given to them if they are currently in the country.

Embassies

Swiss Embassy
16-18 Montagu Place
London W1H 2BQ.
Tel: (020) 7616 6000
Email: vertretung@lon.rep.admin.ch
Web: http://www.swissembassy.org.uk

British Embassy
Thunstrasse 50
3000 Bern.
Tel: 031 359 7700
Web: http://www.britishembassy-berne.ch/

Major UK companies in Switzerland:

Barclays Bank, ICL, ICI, Laura Ashley, Proctor & Gamble, Prudential, Rank Xerox, Shell, Thomson, Thorn EMI.

Language courses

French

Berlitz: 9–13 Grosvenor Street, London W1A 3BZ. Tel: (020) 7915 0909. In Lausanne: Tel: 021 312 5304.

Inlingua, 28 Rotton Park Road, Birmingham B16 9JL. Tel: (0121) 454 0204.

French language and culture courses are held each summer at the universities of Geneva, Lausanne and Neuchétel. Information about these may be obtained from the Swiss National Tourist Office, Swiss Centre, Swiss Court, London W1V 8EE. Tel (020) 7734 1921.

German

Ferienkurs der Stadt Winterthur, Baccegglіweg 22, Winterthur. Tel: 021 22 67 78.

Also see addresses listed for France, Germany and Italy.

Other useful contacts

Anglo-Swiss Society, Mr C H Bruggmann (Secretary), 14 Salisbury House, 3 Drummond Gate, London SW1V 2HJ. Tel: (020) 7233 8607.

British-Swiss Chamber of Commerce, Freiestrasse 155, CH 8032 Zürich.

Tel: 01 422 31 31 Fax: 01 422 32 44

Swiss National Tourist Office, Swiss Centre, Swiss Court, London W1V 3HG. Tel: (020) 7734 1921.

Swissair, Swiss Centre, 10 Wardour Street, London W1. Tel: 0845 6010956.

Switzerland Hotels (reservations office), Archgate Centre, 823a High Road, London N12. Tel: (020) 8446 1306.

Useful publications

Liste des Associations Professionals et Economiques de la Suisse (List of Professional and Trade Associations in Switzerland), Office Syndicat de l'Industrie, Postfach 2170, 3011 Bern. Tel: 031 350 21 11.

Living and Working in Switzerland, David Hampshire (Survival Handbook, 7th ed. 1999). 396pp paperback.

6

Jobs Across National Boundaries

WORKING IN THE DIPLOMATIC SERVICE

What is the overall potential?

Working for HM Government has always been one of the traditional ways of working abroad. Overall, however, the opportunities to work abroad in this way are very small. The Diplomatic Service recruits no more than about 300 personnel each year, and this includes all grades such as the Secretarial Branch, Executive Branch and Clerical Branch.

In addition to this, personnel are rarely recruited and then posted overseas immediately. It may take some years to receive a posting to a British Embassy or High Commission, and even then the choice of countries may be limited.

In the case of most European countries the requirement for staff overseas is now lower than in the past. However, the work of commercial sections in most embassies has become increasingly important. Should EU political union occur, then the future role of embassies and consulates would become uncertain.

How do you apply?

Applications for some jobs are accepted at any time. Applications for others are only accepted when vacancies arise. If you are interested in the possibilities then there are two main bodies which recruit for the diplomatic service:

Civil Service Commission
Whitehall
London SW1.
Tel:(020) 7270 3000

(Recruits for most jobs in the Administrative, Clerical and Executive Branches.)

Recruitment Section

Personnel Command
Foreign and Commonwealth Office
1 Palace Street
London SW1E 5HE.
Tel: (020) 7270 1500
Fax: (020) 7839 2417
Email: pmd.fco@gtnet.gov.uk

(Recruits for other posts, including Legal, Communications and Secretarial Branches.)

ARE THERE OPENINGS IN THE EUROPEAN UNION?

What is the overall potential?

Working for the European Union itself is becoming one of the most popular ways of working in Europe. Although the most well known EU institutions are in Brussels or Luxembourg, there are EU offices all over Europe, including the UK, in such places as Karlsruhe (Germany) and Ispra (Italy). The total number of people employed is approximately 22,000.

Many vacancies are available annually, but competition is also very strong. There are no national quotas so suitably qualified people from any EU country can apply for every vacancy. The majority of the vacancies are administrative or clerical, but there is also a requirement for interpreters, translators and scientific or technical personnel.

Employing institutions

There are six separate employers within the EU:

- Council of the European Union
- European Parliament
- Court of Justice
- Court of Auditors
- Economic and Social Committee of the European Communities
- The European Commission.

The Commission of the European Communities employs over 75 per cent of the EU workforce. There are over 30 departments within the Commission, including 23 Directorates-General.

Grading system

All jobs with the EU are categorised according to a grading system. The system which applies to the Commission is shown in Figure 13.

Category	Function	Qualifications required
A	Policy and administrative work	Degree
LA	Interpreters and translators	Degree
B	Executive work	Minimum 2 'A' levels
C	Secretarial and clerical work	Minimum 5 GCSEs
D	Support and manual work	Proof of completion of secondary education

Fig. 13. Grading system of the European Commission.

Personnel within each category are usually recruited to the lowest grade of each category (*eg* D4 or B5), and then move upwards by promotion and applying for jobs in open competitions (*eg* to D1 or B1 eventually). It is also possible to be promoted to a higher category, for example C to B.

How initial recruitment is made

How to find out about vacancies

The majority of vacancies in the EU, except the most senior, are filled

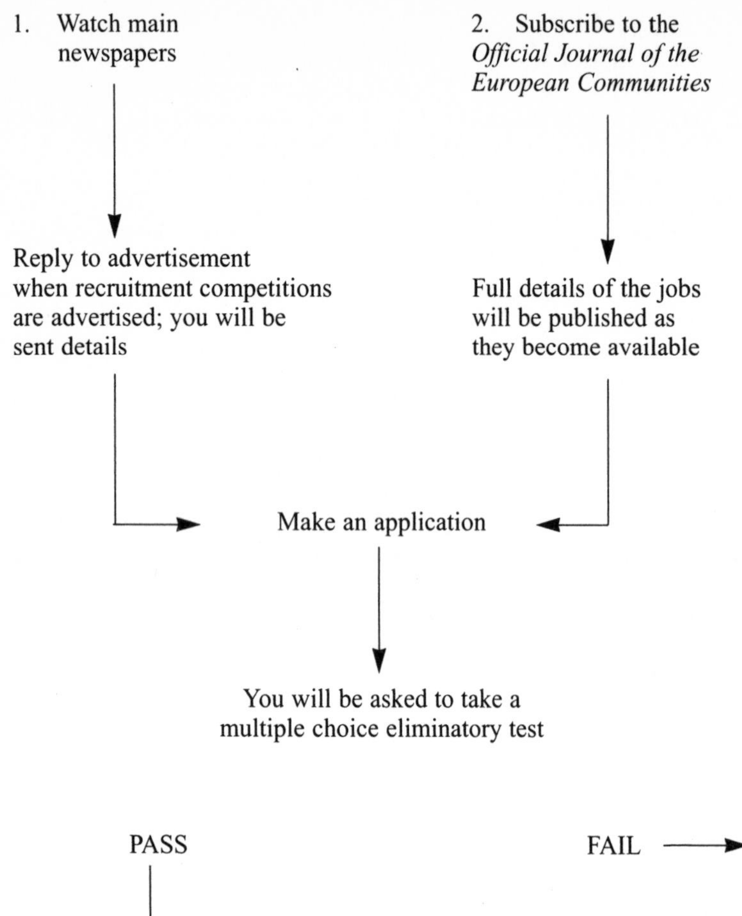
1. Watch main newspapers
2. Subscribe to the *Official Journal of the European Communities*
Reply to advertisement when recruitment competitions are advertised; you will be sent details
Full details of the jobs will be published as they become available
Make an application
You will be asked to take a multiple choice eliminatory test

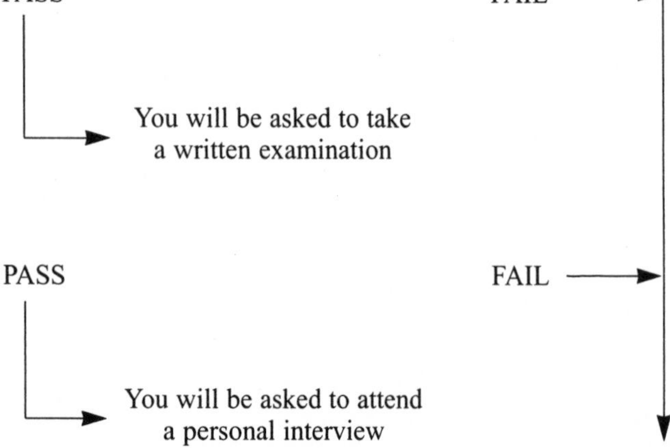
PASS
FAIL
You will be asked to take a written examination
PASS
FAIL
You will be asked to attend a personal interview

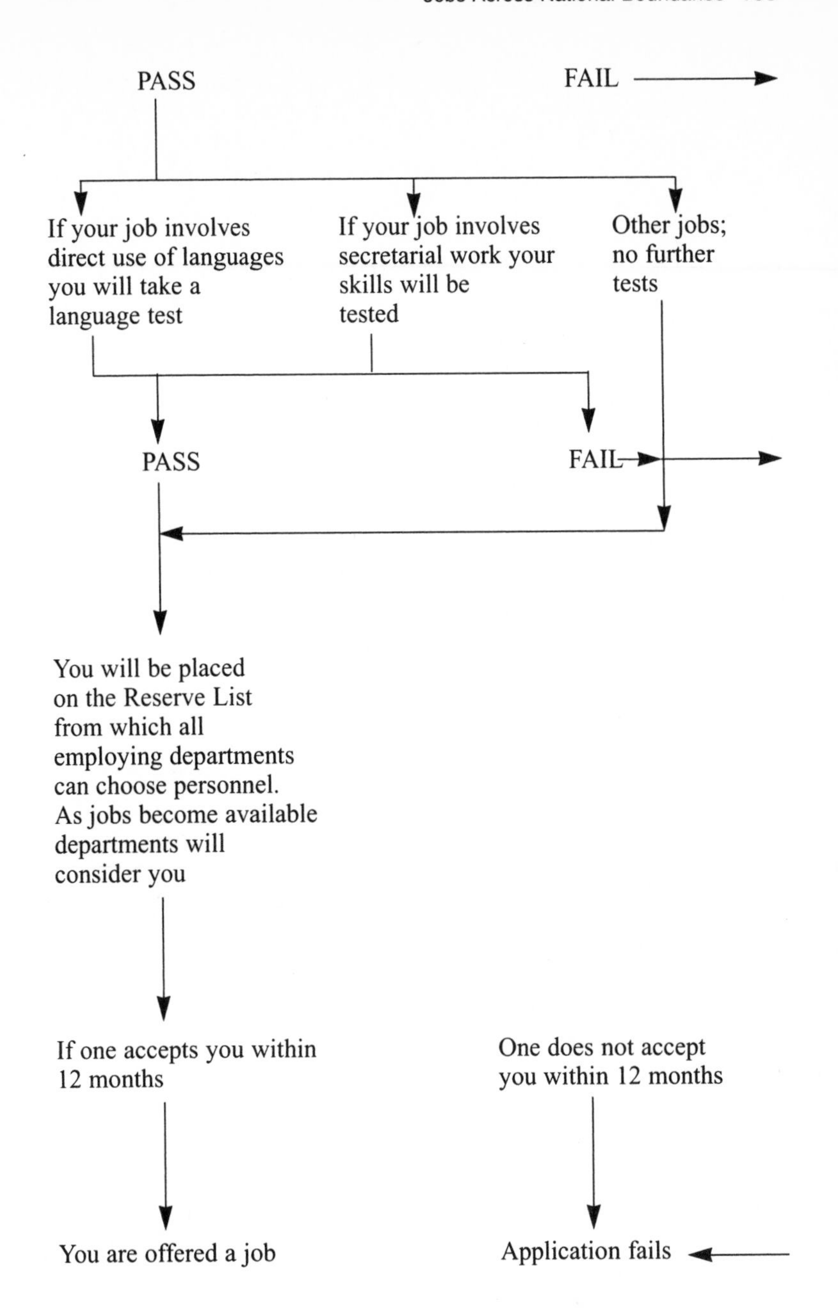

Fig. 14. How to get a job with one of the European Union institutions.

by a method of open competition. Any eligible applicant can apply, but only when vacancies are advertised. Each EU institution recruits separately but follows a similar procedure.

Whenever staff are required for a particular category, the opportunities will be advertised in the main newspapers of the EU and the *Official Journal of the European Communities*, which is available on subscription. The *Official Journal* gives full details of the jobs available and the qualifications which are necessary.

What qualifications will I need?

- academic qualifications according to appropriate category, as above
- maximum age limit 35, 32 for some posts
- two years' experience in similar work
- most jobs require fluency in one Community language and at least knowledge of another. The EU recognises academic qualifications from every EU country.

What is the procedure?

The application procedure is made up of a number of different stages and can be undertaken in any of the official EU languages and in any of the EU countries. The procedure is shown in Figure 14, although it can vary slightly according to the job being applied for.

The procedure can take up to 12 months. Candidates who are successful in these examinations are placed on the Reserve List. Once placed on this list you are eligible to be offered a job by one of the departments; a placing on this list is not a guarantee of a job. About 80 per cent of applicants on the list are offered jobs, but after 12 months on the list (which can very occasionally be extended) your application lapses.

What are working conditions like?

EU staff work a 37½ hour week and are entitled to 24-30 days paid holiday. Salaries are paid according to an EU scale rated in Euros, but weighted to the costs in the country of employment. Salaries are taxed at a special EU tax rate and not taxed in the country concerned. Social Security contributions for pension and sickness insurance are deducted.

The EU pays a removal and relocation allowance and will also pay school fees at a designated international school for the employee's children.

Further information

Further information on recruitment to the European Commission, and contact addresses for the other EU institutions, can be obtained from:

The Commission of the European Communities
8 Storey's Gate
London SW1P 2AT.
Tel: (020) 7973 1992

SEASONAL AND HOLIDAY JOBS AND EXCHANGES

Prior to the granting of rights to work in any of the EU countries, special seasonal and holiday job and exchange programmes were the main way of working in Europe. Nowadays, there are fewer of these special programmes; those wanting summer work abroad are able to take any job they can find in any EU country.

There are, however, various ways of getting a short taster of work in Europe. These are primarily for young people and for fixed periods of between three months and one year. Wages are usually low and often of pocket money level, if that. Some of the main possibilities are listed below.

Working as an au pair or nanny

Au pairs are usually women aged 18-27 (some countries will accept men) who live with a family for a year to experience the local way of life. They look after children and may do a little housework, depending on the arrangement. Often the au pair has to study locally, usually a language.

Au pairing is customary in all European countries to a greater or lesser extent, and is particularly popular in France, Germany and Scandinavia. You can find your own job by advertising in a newspaper in the country in question, but there are many agencies in the UK which will arrange placements. More details about au pairing and a list of agencies can be found in the book *Working as an Au Pair* which is available from How to Books.

Nannying may involve similar work, but is a career which usually demands qualifications and pays more than the pocket money au pairs receive.

Voluntary and charity work

Most of the European countries offer opportunities to carry out voluntary and charity work. This might include working with the old, young or disabled, or working in conservation.

Voluntary and charity work usually pays little, if anything. Sometimes volunteers are paid expenses, a wage at local rates, or receive a grant. Most schemes provide travel, accommodation and food but in a few the volunteer is responsible for these.

There are several specialist organisations arranging voluntary and charity work but the following work in Europe:

International Voluntary Service, Old Hall, East Bergholt, Colchester CO7 6TQ. Tel: (01206) 298215.

United Nations: UNA Exchange, Temple of Peace, Cathays Park, Cardiff CF10 3AP. Tel: (029) 2022 3088.

Further information on opportunities for voluntary and charity work, and a list of organisations, is given in *Finding Voluntary Work Abroad* from How to Books.

Exchange programmes

Several countries have exchange programmes which permit those working in a particular industry, or students, to have a period of work experience in another European country. Most of the schemes are for young people aged 18-25. For example a programme exists for students studying technical subjects to undertake holiday work in the Netherlands. Another programme is for those working in the hotel trade to spend a few months working in a French hotel or restaurant.

The main advantage of these programmes is that they find a placement for each applicant and also deal with the bureaucracy of residence permits, etc.

It is worth asking the embassy of the appropriate country if any programmes exist. However, many of these schemes are administered by the Central Bureau and described in their annual publication *Working Holidays*.

Central Bureau for Educational Visits and Exchanges
The British Council
10 Spring Gardens
London SW1A 2BN.
Tel: (020) 7389 4004
Fax: (020) 7389 4426
Email: centralbureau@britishcouncil.org

The Central Bureau also administers the **Young Workers Exchange Programme** which finances working exchanges. If your college or employer does not already participate in the YWEP, it is possible to apply for a grant to organise your own working exchange.

Stagiaire Programme

The EU has an **Administrative Trainee Programme**, sometimes known as the Stagiaire Programme, by which those under 30 with a university degree can work with an EU office for a period of three to five months each year. This is as work experience rather than with a view to a career with the EU. The work is paid. Competition for places is heavy and those who have studied European affairs, or who work in related fields, have the best chance of success. Full details of the scheme can be obtained from the European Commission.

At one time an organised working holiday or exchange used to be the easiest way of working in Europe. It may still be for non-EU countries. However, nowadays it is often easier to go-as-you-please and find your own job on the way.

7

Living in Europe

Moving overseas is often considered a carefree business. However, although your job is likely to be a challenge in itself, the procedure of actually moving can be more challenging still! There is much to be said for planning every stage — not only for your departure but also for your return. A growing number of European expatriates now actually move permanently. It is always useful though to keep open the option to return, perhaps for a period of two or three years, until you have made a final decision that continental Europe really is for you.

Although the countries of the EU have simplified or removed the barriers of work and residence permits the cultural differences still exist and should not be underestimated. The way of life is still very different in the individual countries.

GETTING THERE

What's the best way to travel to Europe?

Few European employers will provide any sort of contribution to travelling costs for those taking a job on the continent. After all, they could employ a native of their country. The cost must be considered, especially if you expect to return to the UK; perhaps your children will remain at school here, or you may wish to return for a holiday. In some countries tax regulations may allow such travel to be deducted as a business expense.

Going by air

Cheap fares are often last minute deals or, conversely, must be prebooked long in advance. Regular tickets may cost three or four times this price.

The cheap flights on offer to a popular holiday country like Spain are not usually available elsewhere in Europe. Flights within Europe are the most costly, mile for mile, anywhere in the world.

Surface transport

Car and rail transport are often little cheaper than air when the cost of fuel, road tolls, food and accommodation en route is added. Coach is by far the cheapest way of travelling Europe-wide, but journey times are still substantial.

Taking your car to Europe

One of the advantages of travelling to your post by car is that you will already have personal transport on arrival. Whether you wish to do this or not is a matter of personal choice. Remember that all the European countries drive on the right, causing extra difficulties when using a right-hand drive UK model car. It may also be difficult to resell or part-exchange abroad. Consider also if servicing facilities will be available.

Importing a car into EU countries

You have a right to import your own car into any EU country without payment of any duties or taxes. The conditions on this vary but are usually that:

- the car must not be new
- it must have been registered in your name for six months
- it must be registered duty-paid in another EU country
- only one car per person is permitted duty-free and commercial vehicles are not eligible.

Individual countries are allowed to impose their own import procedures rather than any overall EU rules. These should be checked in advance, but it is not usually necessary to get a permit in advance. After a period of grace all countries will insist that the car is registered and road-taxed under their own national system. Your car must meet all local safety standards especially as regards emission control.

Importing a car into non-EU countries

All European countries outside the EU permit private car imports, but all charge a high import duty. You should check this before moving as it is invariably cheaper to buy a car locally.

Driving licences

A UK driving licence is valid in most European countries and can be used there for a period up to 12 months. It can be exchanged for a local licence without having to take another driving test and it is preferable to do this on arrival.

If your proposed job involves driving, do check in advance, as minimum driving ages and vehicle groups are not the same in every country, even though EU countries use the same driving licence form.

Further information

Information on vehicle imports and licences is usually available from the respective embassy.

Taking your personal possessions

You are entitled to import all your personal possessions, household furniture and household effects into any EU country without having to pay import taxes or duties. The regulations under which this can be done are different in every EU country and should be checked with the relevant embassy or consulate in advance.

Business equipment, and tools or equipment to be used in your profession, may not be admitted tax free. VAT at the appropriate local rate is usually chargeable although, conversely, you may reclaim UK VAT paid on export.

Most non-EU countries restrict tax-free imports to personal possessions, *eg*, clothing only. Enquiries should be made in advance as to what will be allowed.

What insurance will I need?

As part of your removal procedure it is essential to make sure that any insurance policies (household, motor etc) are transferred as necessary. At the time of writing, insurance companies do not usually insure residents in other countries and you must take out insurance with a company in your new country. In due course, British insurance companies may insure vehicles and property in Europe, and vice versa. At present though this is usually not possible, except in certain cases, such as holiday homes.

WHAT LANGUAGE ABILITY WILL I NEED?

Do I need to speak the language?

English is an important world language and it is quite possible to travel as a tourist in many countries without speaking the local language. However, if you intend to work in a country it is, with very few exceptions, essential to speak the local language. Sometimes menial workers may manage without the local language, and executives may find that their colleagues speak good English anyway, but the need to speak the local language should not be underestimated.

Many European nationals, such as the Danes, speak English much better than is realised, but sometimes English language ability is over-estimated. Not all French people speak any English, for example.

Country	Main language	English spoken?
France	French	Little or none
Germany	German	Some people speak good English
Belgium	French/Flemish	Widely in Brussels, little elsewhere
Netherlands	Dutch	Quite good English spoken
Denmark	Danish	Good English spoken
Spain	Spanish	Only in tourist areas
Portugal	Portuguese	A little in tourist areas, Spanish sometimes understood
Italy	Italian	English usually not spoken
Greece	Greek	Only a little English (and German) in Athens and tourist areas
Switzerland	French/German/Italian	Occasionally
Austria	German	English usually not spoken
Norway	Norwegian	A little
Sweden	Swedish	A little
Finland	Finnish/Swedish	A little
Eastern Europe	Varies	A little English (and German)

Fig. 15. Who speaks what in Europe.

Learning foreign languages

It is always better to start learning a language before leaving home. However, it can be easier once abroad and you are immersed in the local language. Note that formal tuition courses are usually more expensive once abroad.

Consider the following methods:

- Audio cassette courses. Usually inexpensive, but there is no opportunity to practise. Obtain from bookshops, or through magazine/newspaper advertisements.

- Evening classes. Inexpensive, but usually aimed at holidaymakers. Limited selection of languages. For details refer to your local further education college.

- Commercial schools. A quick way to learn but costly and geared mainly for business people. For details see *Yellow Pages*.

- Residential courses abroad. Usually held at universities in Europe during the summer vacation. Are generally time-consuming.

- Commercial schools in Europe. A quick way to learn but can be costly. Check that the school is reputable. Several schools around Europe are run by:
  Berlitz International
  9–13 Grosvenor Street
  London W1A 3BZ.
  Tel: (020) 7915 0909

FINDING A HOME

It is always advisable to find a home before leaving to take up your job. In some countries accommodation is hard to find and expensive — especially Italy, Austria, Switzerland and Scandinavia. Temporary accommodation in a hotel can also be prohibitively costly, although both France and Spain are easier on the wallet.

European employers do not usually provide accommodation or pay towards it as a matter of course. Usually only hotel or farm employees receive live-in accommodation. If employers help with finding accommodation it will be as a favour which must be requested; it is rarely customary.

Accommodation can be located by:

- using estate agents in the respective country. Refer to their *Yellow Pages*
- classified advertisements in newspapers. Refer to the publications listed in Chapter 5.

Property leases or purchases are according to the law of each European country and differ greatly. There are no EU laws or regulations on this. In most European countries property agents are allowed to charge a fee to a buyer or tenant (often equivalent to two months' rent), though not all do. In every country, management and running charges for apartment blocks are much higher than in the UK, due to the different way that communal property is rented and owned.

SOCIAL SECURITY AND HEALTH PROVISION IN EUROPE

Social security in the EU

The social security system throughout the EU is already well integrated. This has little to do with recent developments; the system has been well integrated for several years. The main advantage of the system is that it is portable. Your social security contributions in one EU country entitle you to social security benefits in another.

As long as your social security contributions record is fully paid up in any one of the EU countries, you will be entitled to social security benefits in any of the others. So, for example, if you work in the UK and then move to France to work, you can claim French benefits from your UK record. If you then move to Germany you can claim German benefits, using both your UK and French record. If you then move back to the UK you can claim UK benefits based on records in all countries.

Registering for social security

Always check on arrival in your new country whether you need to register for social security. In some states your employer will do this and take deductions directly from your wage. In others you will need to register at a social security office and obtain a social security card. For example, in Germany, you must obtain a **Krankenschein** each year to present to a doctor or hospital should it become necessary.

Some countries expect to see evidence that your UK social security record is fully paid up. Form E104 satisfies this requirement and it can be obtained from the Department of Social Security (DSS) Overseas Branch before leaving the UK.

What benefits are available?
The range of social security benefits varies from country to country, but most provide at least:

- unemployment benefits
- retirement pensions
- industrial accident insurance
- maternity benefits
- medical treatment.

Some countries handle medical treatment separately from their other social security benefits. In these countries medical insurance contributions will be collected separately from social security.

When do you become eligible?
As soon as you start working and paying contributions, you and your dependent family usually become entitled to health benefits. However, there is often a qualifying period for other benefits, which varies from country to country from between three and six months. Contributions in any other EU country can be counted towards this.

Rates of benefit
Benefits in all EU countries are paid as a percentage of former salary, rather than a flat rate as in the UK. For example, unemployment benefit in France is paid at 40 per cent of former salary.

Transferring unemployment benefit
Those unemployed in the UK can transfer their unemployment benefit to an EU country whilst living there and looking for a job. This is possible if you have been claiming benefit for four weeks or more. In order to do this ask your unemployment benefit office for Form E303.

On arrival in the appropriate EU country, register at the local social security office. Outside France, Germany and Italy the E303 must be sent to a nominated office. You can then receive benefit at the UK rate for up to three months. Note: in some countries local offices may not be familiar with this procedure and some persistence will be required!

Non-EU European countries
Non-EU European countries have similar health and social security systems to those described above. Deductions will usually be made from your salary and you will be entitled to the same benefits as locals. The

main difference here is that your contributions record is not portable between that country and the UK and vice versa.

In this situation, if you want to maintain a complete UK social security contributions record, you must arrange to pay contributions to the UK DSS. However, these will not entitle you to any benefits (*eg* free health treatment) in the non-EU country.

Further information

Further information can be obtained from:

The Department of Social Security (DSS)
Overseas Branch
Newcastle Upon Tyne
NE98 1YX.
Tel: 0191 218 7777

Ask for booklet SA29.

Hospitals and health provision

What are healthcare standards like?

Generally, hospital treatment is considered as good as or better than the UK in Germany, France, Benelux and Scandinavia. Only in Greece, Portugal, parts of Spain and eastern Europe are they likely to be inferior. In all cases local standards apply. English-speaking doctors are available only in some places.

National health services

Few countries have national health services like the UK where all treatment is free. Most hospitals in Europe are run privately and all treatment *must be paid for*. However, most countries, whether in the EU or not, run a **state health insurance scheme** which may or may not be part of the overall social security system. Foreign residents who pay into this are entitled to the same benefits (no better and no worse) as locals.

Sometimes these contributions are made by the employer, or employee, or both; sometimes they are managed by a state organisation, sometimes a private insurance company. In some countries, such as Germany, those on high incomes can take private health insurance instead of the state scheme, or both, or need not have any insurance at all.

Be sure to check the details. It is usually necessary to register at a **sickness insurance office** and obtain a **medical card** or **book of vouchers** to entitle you to treatment. In most countries you must make a claim from the insurance scheme; treatment is not automatically free. In others

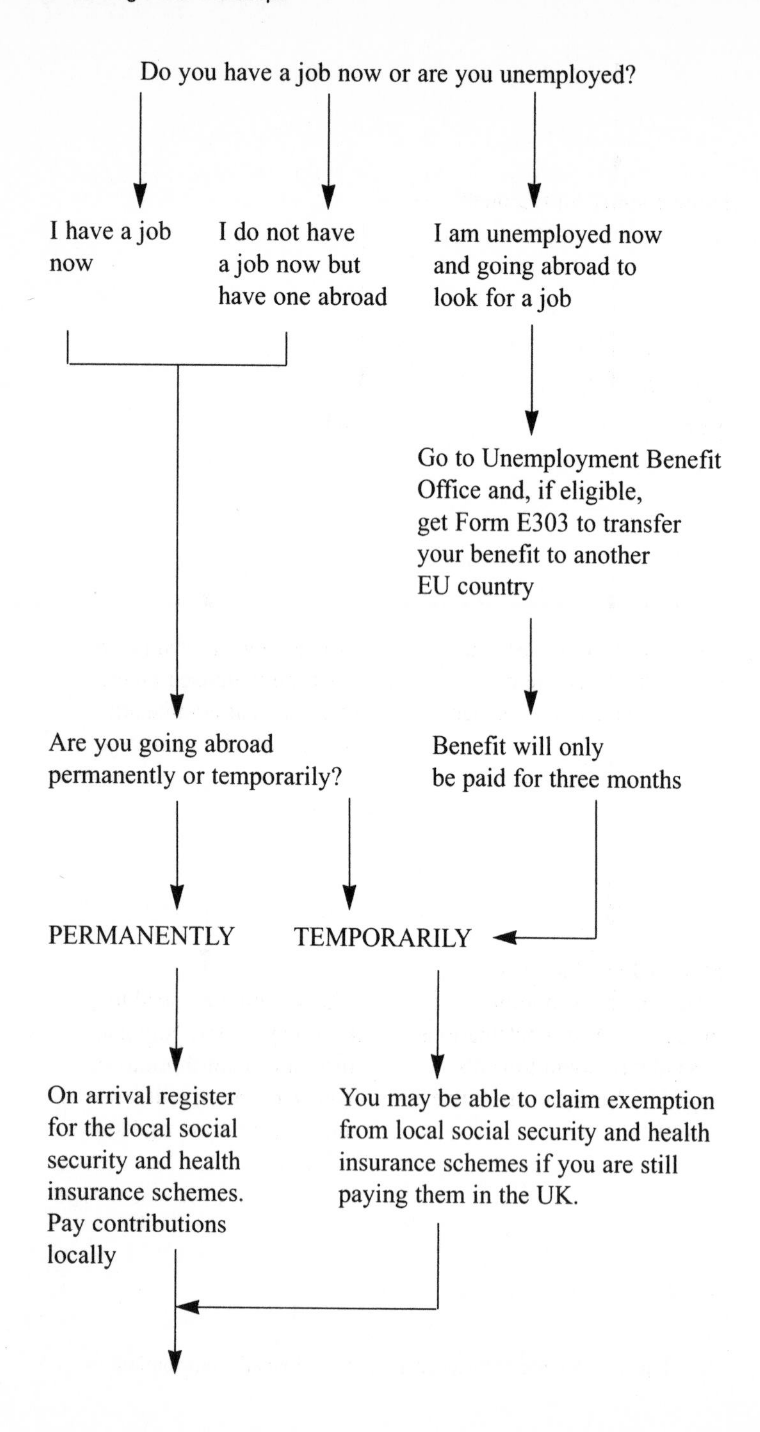
Do you have a job now or are you unemployed?
I have a job now
I do not have a job now but have one abroad
I am unemployed now and going abroad to look for a job
Go to Unemployment Benefit Office and, if eligible, get Form E303 to transfer your benefit to another EU country
Are you going abroad permanently or temporarily?
Benefit will only be paid for three months
PERMANENTLY
TEMPORARILY
On arrival register for the local social security and health insurance schemes. Pay contributions locally
You may be able to claim exemption from local social security and health insurance schemes if you are still paying them in the UK.

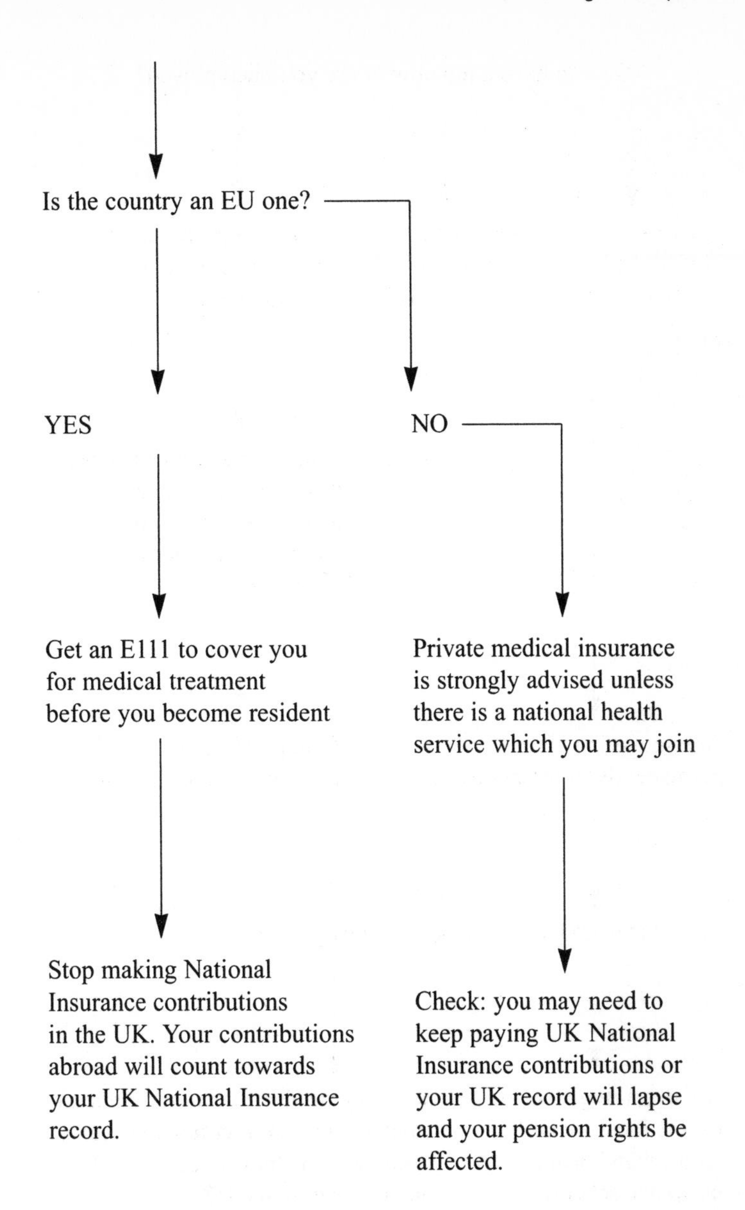

Fig. 16. Dealing with social security and health contributions.

it is necessary to pay for treatment and then claim your outlay back from the insurance scheme.

In some countries, state insurance only covers a percentage of the cost of treatment (such as 70 or 90 per cent). You must pay the balance or take private insurance to make up the difference.

Take form E111

Form E111 is available from main post offices in the UK. It will entitle you to the same free or reduced-cost medical treatment as locals, where available, in any EU country, in the period between your arrival abroad and registering for a local medical insurance scheme. It is the same form as used by tourists to entitle them to treatment elsewhere in the EU. An E111 is only valid as long as you live in the UK, *ie* until you become resident in your new country.

USING MONEY AND BANKS

Importing and exporting money

Money can be transferred to any European country quite easily. There are no limits on the amount of money which can be exported from the UK. However, some countries demand that imports over a certain amount have to be declared to their customs.

Many countries impose limits on the amount of local currency that can be exported, or insist that it is declared. Check into this before leaving, as local restrictions may result in your earnings in another country being trapped there.

What currency should I be paid in?

All the currencies of western Europe are freely convertible and expatriates need not usually be too concerned about being paid in the local currency. However, do remember that exchange rate fluctuations may affect the value of what you earn compared to the cost of living in the UK. The new pan European currency, the Euro, is scheduled to replace all national currencies in most of the EU countries during 2002.

If working in eastern Europe, you may wish to be paid wholly or partly in a hard currency (usually US dollars) as the local currency may not be freely convertible and, effectively, be worthless outside that country. Due to a shortage of hard currency in these places, making such a request may make it harder to obtain a suitable job.

Opening a bank account

To open a local bank account, ask your UK bank manager for a referral or just call into a bank abroad. Most banks will insist that you have a residence permit and a permanent address in that country before they will grant you a full account. In most countries cheque books, credit cards, overdrafts, loans and mortgages are only granted after a satisfactory period of banking — sometimes five years.

Further information

All the main UK banks have expatriate departments. Addresses are in the further information section.

TAXATION WHILE ABROAD

What are the levels of tax?

Information on rates of taxation appears in Chapter 5. There are currently no plans to standardise income tax rates across the EU.

Tax rates are not the only thing to consider when thinking about a move. Some countries have greater allowances than the UK, so although the rate may be higher you are actually taxed less. For example, Germany permits travel to work as a tax-deductible expense, which isn't allowed in the UK. In all countries tax is applied on a progressive, sliding scale.

Registering for taxation

It is advisable to register with the local tax authorities when you arrive. Do not assume the employer will do it. The address of the appropriate authority can be found in the local *Yellow Pages*. In some places (such as Germany) you may not be able to get a residence permit without first having obtained a tax card.

Systems of income tax vary from country to country but are either:

- **Pay as you earn (PAYE)**: As the UK where tax is deducted by your employer.

- **Annual return**: You must complete a tax return each year and submit it to the tax authorities. You then receive a tax bill for payment, usually in instalments.

In almost every European country the tax year runs January-December, not April-April as in the UK.

Leaving the UK Inland Revenue behind

Leaving the UK and working in another country does not automatically render you liable to tax in that country, nor does it allow you to escape UK tax automatically. You can be physically resident and earning your income in a foreign country, but still regarded as resident in the UK for tax purposes by the Inland Revenue.

In order to cease to be liable for UK tax you usually have to:

- be based abroad for at least one full tax year
- not return to the UK for more than three months in any one year
- be employed in work that is wholly undertaken abroad (business trips back to the UK are allowed)
- not have property available for your use in the UK.

However, situations vary and it is up to the Inland Revenue to decide if they consider you resident in the UK for tax purposes, and liable to tax on your overseas earnings, or not. Be sure to consult with them carefully before moving. In some cases it can take up to three years to receive confirmation that you are not considered resident in the UK for tax purposes.

Becoming liable for foreign taxation

Taxation regulations vary from one European country to another. Some countries will consider you liable for tax on every penny earned from arrival. Others will not apply this until you have been resident for a certain period. Some countries will tax you only on income earned in that country, whereas others tax on the basis of 'world income'. In any case, it is usually advisable to register with the local tax office on arrival to avoid contravening local regulations. Local accountancy help can then be sought at your convenience.

Double taxation

Unlike the social security system there is very little cooperation between the revenue authorities, even of the EU countries. The only system of cooperation that exists is that of **double taxation**. Some European countries have double tax agreements with the UK.

The principles of double taxation mean that if you have income in both countries (for example, a wage in Germany and bank interest in UK), you will not have to pay tax twice on the same income — once in each country — but only in the country where you are considered resident or where the income arises. Sometimes it may actually be necessary to pay the tax twice and then reclaim it from either or both countries.

Returning to the UK

Returning to the UK should always be planned from a tax point of view and it is advisable to plan for this even if, at the time of leaving, you do not intend to return. The most important consideration is that you will be considered resident in the UK for tax purposes from the very day you arrive back. In other words, you do not have to establish residence back in the UK as it was necessary to establish residence out of the UK.

This will generally mean that all subsequent income will be subject to UK tax. It also means that you are entitled to a full year's UK tax allowances, regardless of how far into the tax year you return.

Careful selection of a return date can, therefore, result in some tax benefits. There can also be benefits in deciding when any end-of-contract bonus is paid, in order to choose whether it should be taxed under the UK tax system or that in the relevant European country, depending on which will result in the least tax.

Finally, note that returning earlier than expected from a job overseas can be costly in terms of becoming liable for extra tax. This could happen if, for example, you fail to qualify as non-resident in the UK for tax purposes when this, and a subsequent tax saving, was anticipated. As in all tax situations expert advice can help here; it is also now possible to insure against such extra costs.

Further information

Further information should be obtained from your local Inland Revenue Office (see telephone directory). Ask for booklets IR6 and IR20.

Bank expatriate services can also help.

REQUIREMENTS FOR CHILDREN AND EDUCATION

Residence for children in EU countries

In all the EU countries children are entitled to move and live with their parents as a matter of right. They may require a separate residence permit or identity card but it will be granted automatically. On reaching the age of majority (18-21 depending on the country) they will be entitled to residence in their own right.

Residence for children in non-EU countries

The position in non-EU countries differs from place to place. Children are invariably allowed to live with their parents up until the age of majority. After that they may not be allowed to live there unless they can obtain a job which will render them eligible for a work permit of their own. Having said this, some countries (like Sweden) will accept application for citizenship after five years' residence, which may be a solution if the children wish to adopt their new country.

Arranging education

There are three main options when going to live in Europe:

Boarding school in the UK

This will result in separation of the family and it can be expensive. Not many European employers will pay towards it. Details of boarding schools in the UK are available from:

Independent Schools Information Service (ISIS)
35–37 Grosvenor Gardens
London SW1W 0BS.
Tel: (020) 7798 1500

Local schools

EU citizens can use state schools in any EU country, and this is free of charge where the same schooling is free to nationals. Children will usually be accepted into state schools in most other countries, but a fee may be charged. However, standards vary and no country makes any provision for children who do not speak the local language.

The embassy of the appropriate country can usually advise on the procedure. In the case of non-EU countries it is usually necessary to gain permission from the Ministry of Education.

International schools/private schools in Europe

There are international schools and private schools all over Europe which offer tuition in English. Some, but not all, also offer a UK curriculum and UK examinations (GCSE and 'A' level). Fees can be high and not many employers will contribute. Details of possible schools can be found in *The Directory of International Schools*.

Higher education

Generally, all the main universities in Europe will accept foreign residents. Under EU regulations a degree from one is considered equivalent to a degree from a university in any other EU country. Few countries have higher education that is totally free and study must largely be funded by students, parents, loans or scholarships.

ADJUSTING TO DAILY LIFE ABROAD

Going to live in another country is bound to be an upheaval, and the small details can be as troublesome as more substantial matters like health insurance and taxation. It is impossible to cover them all here, but some of the main concerns raised by expatriates are:

- Language. Are you prepared to learn?
- Climate. Can you live *and* work in a hot/cold climate?
- Clothes. Can you get clothing to suit your tastes locally?
- Property. Is local property affordable and to your liking?
- Furnishings. Can you easily get these locally? Is there anything you need or would like to take?
- Food. Is British-style food available? Must you have it anyway?
- Cost of living. What is the price of utilities, transport etc?
- Travelling to work. Will you have to commute a long distance? How much will it cost?
- Social life. How easy is it to make friends? What opportunities are there for entertainment or sport?

Plus some other matters which should not be taken for granted:

- political situation
- economic situation
- crime levels
- personal freedom.

Further help

UK embassies and consulates
UK missions can only help with official matters like passport renewals and voting rights. Some will offer general help and advice to residents, but on an official basis. In an emergency they can help make arrangements, *eg* for hospitals or repatriation, but cannot pay for anything.

Neighbours and colleagues at work
There are very few countries whose citizens are not flattered to have foreigners living or working with them, so neighbours and colleagues at work can often be a good source of help. But — be sure to approach them properly. In some countries (like Germany) you would always

address your neighbour by his surname and be sure to shake hands on meeting. In other countries, like Italy, your neighbours might be offended if you are so formal.

Friendship clubs
In a few popular destinations there are expatriate groups you can join. Check in local newspapers.

Hotels and bars
In most chief cities of the world there will be a hotel or bar where British expatriates congregate. A good source of advice and possible further job contacts.

Tourist offices
A useful source of information and English-speaking help. Most tourist offices will be pleased to help foreigners, even if residents.

Police
In some countries the police are helpful, in others they are best avoided unless in an emergency.

Town hall
Some municipal authorities are helpful to foreigners, others resent them. Much depends on finding a friendly official in the right department!

Clubs and newsletters
You might keep in touch with the expatriate life and issues with a club or newsletter like *Home and Away*.

8

How to Get Started

Britain's membership of the European Union has brought many gradual changes. One of the most valuable opportunities has been available for many years now, and means that British citizens can just take off and look for a new job in Europe.

Moving from Manchester to Munich overnight may now be entirely possible, but it is rarely advisable nor necessarily simple. The best advice must be to plan carefully and thoroughly, but at least EU citizens have the right to move around if they so choose. And that is certainly a right worth having, and worth thinking about seriously.

Planning, though, should not become an end in itself. Many, many people who set out to work abroad eventually find themselves doing something completely different to that which was planned. They may end up in a different job. They may even end up in a different country!

If you want to work outside the EU, then do accept that the process of finding a job will probably be as difficult as it ever was. You *must* plan right down to the smallest detail. Remember that, by and large, these countries won't want you unless you have something to offer.

The following action plan is a brief refresher to the main, practical ways of finding a job in Europe.

PERSONAL ACTION PLAN 2

1. Decide what job(s) you wish to do.

2. Decide which country(ies) you prefer.

3. Check for any vacancies in the UK newspapers.

4. Check for any vacancies in the newspapers of the country concerned.

5. Check relevant magazines, journals and bulletins.

6. Use the UK Employment Service and EURES.

7. Use the state employment service of the relevant country direct, if possible.

8. Use private employment agencies in the UK and Europe.

9. Approach embassies, chambers of commerce, professional associations and trade directories for details of possible employers to whom you may make speculative applications.

10. Make applications from the UK first.

11. If necessary, and permissible, travel to the relevant country and follow up leads.

12. Make applications. Repeat the procedure until job is found. If necessary return to step 1 and repeat the procedure with other jobs or other countries.

13. Before accepting any job offer check out work and residence permit regulations.

14. Accept job and travel out!

Further Information

FURTHER READING

Books and directories

Buying a Home Abroad, David Hampshire (Survival Books, 1998).
CEPEC Recruitment Guide (CEPEC).
The Daily Telegraph Guide to Working Abroad, Godfrey Golzen (Kogan Page, 2000).
The EC/EU Fact Book, Alex Rooney (Kogan Page, 1997).
The European Community: A Guide to the Maze, S. A. Budd and A. Jones (Kogan Page, 1994).
Harrap's Five Language Business Dictionary (English, French, German, Italian, Spanish).
Getting a Job Abroad, Roger Jones (How To Books 5th edn, 1999).
Getting That Job, Joan Fletcher (How To Books, 1997).
How to Study Abroad, Teresa Tinsley (How To Books, 1995).
Living & Working in France, Alan Hart (How To Books, 1998).
Living & Working in Germany, Christine Hall (How To Books, 1995).
Living & Working in Greece, Peter Reynolds (How To Books).
Living & Working in Italy, Amanda Hinton (How To Books, 1999).
Living & Working in the Netherlands, Pat Rush (How To Books, 2000).
Living & Working in Spain, Robert A. C. Richards (How To Books, 1998).
Ostarhild, Edda, *Careers Using Languages* (Kogan Page, 1998).
Teaching Abroad, Roger Jones (How To Books, 1998).
The New European Community Revisited, Loukas Tsoukalis (Oxford University Press, 1997).
The Rough Guide Series: France, Greece, Spain, Portugal, Eastern Europe, Germany, Holland, Belgium and Luxembourg (Rough Guides).
Jupp, Ben *Working Holidays* (Central Bureau, 1999).
Worldwide Volunteering for Young People (How To Books).

Magazines and journals

Official Journal of the European Communities, available from HMSO, 51 Nine Elms Lane, London SW8 5DR. Tel: 0870 6005522.

Connaught Executive Bulletin, 32 Savile Row, London W1X 1AG. Weekly bulletin of senior executive vacancies.

Courier Cadre, 8 rue Duret, F-75783 Paris, France. French directory of executive/professional job vacancies.

De Vacature, PO Box 7, 7200 AA Zutphen, Netherlands. Dutch journal for executives/professionals.

The European Communities Encyclopedia and Directory (Europa Publications, 1999).

European Municipal Directory The Stationery Office Agency, 1999.

Home & Away, Expats House, 29 Lacon Road, London SE22 9HE. Tel: (020) 8299 4987. Monthly magazine covering expatriate matters with vacancies and an availability list for members.

Le Journal de l'Emploi, rue de L'Arquebuse 8, 1204 Geneva. Tel: 022 807 0670. Swiss employment journal.

Overseas Jobs Express, Premier House, Shoreham Airport BN43 5FF. Tel: (01273) 440220. Bi-monthly newspaper for those seeking work overseas, with jobs column.

Position, Postfach 1455, D-82317 Starnberg, Germany. Tel: 08151 7710 Fax: 08151 71190. Specialist vacancy bulletin.

Resident Abroad, 149 Tottenham Court Road, London W1P 9LL. Tel: (020) 7896 2525 Fax: (020) 7896 2222. Monthly magazine for expatriates, giving much financial advice.

Kompass Directories (Kompass Publications). The Kompass directories (published for all main countries) are an authoritative list of industry in that country. Costly to purchase but should be available at all main libraries.

USEFUL ADDRESSES

Barclays Bank plc, Expatriate Dept, 13 Library Place, St Helier, Jersey. Tel: (01534) 87851.

Berlitz International, 9–13 Grosvenor Street, London W1A 3BZ. Tel: (020) 7915 0909.

British Association of Removers, 3 Churchill Court, 58 Station Road, North Harrow, Middx HA2 7SA. Tel: (020) 8861 3331.

BUPA International Sales Office, Provident House, Essex St, London WC2R 3AX.

Career Analysts, Career House, 90 Gloucester Place, London W1H

3HN. Tel: (020) 7935 5452.

Centre for International Briefing, Farnham Castle, Surrey GU9 0AG. Tel: (01252) 721194.

Cepec Consulting Ltd, 13 Hanover Square, London W1R 9HD. Tel: (020) 7629 2266.

Civil Service Commission, Whitehall, London SW1. Tel: (020) 7270 3000.

European Commission, 8 Storey's Gate, London SW1P 3AT. Tel: (020) 7973 1992.

Also:

9 Alva Street, Edinburgh EH2 4PH. Tel: (0131) 225 2058.

4 Cathedral Road, Cardiff CF11 9SG. Tel: (029) 2037 1631.

9/15 Bedford Street, Belfast BT2 7EG. Tel: (028) 9024 0708.

200 rue de la Loi, B-1049 Brussels, Belgium.

Recruitment Unit, 41 rue de la Science, B-1040 Brussels, Belgium. Tel: 02 235 28 49.

Council of European Communities, 175 rue de la Loi, B-1048 Brussels. Tel: 02 285 61 11 Fax: 02 285 73 97.

Department of Social Security Overseas Branch, Newcastle Upon Tyne NE98 1YX. Tel:(0191) 213 5000.

Court of Auditors of the European Communities, 12 rue Alcide de Gasperi, L-1615 Luxembourg. Tel: (352) 43981 Fax: (352) 4393 42 Email: euraud@eca.eu.int

Court of Justice of the European Communities, Boulevard Konrad Adenauer, L-2920 Luxembourg. Tel: (352) 43031 Fax: (352) 4303 2500.

Department of Trade and Industry, 1 Victoria Street, London SW1H 0ET. Tel: (020) 7215 5000.

ECIS (European Council of International Schools), 21 Lavant Street, Petersfield, Hants GU32 3EL. Tel: (01730) 268244 Fax: (01730) 267914 Email: ecis@ecis.org

Economic and Social Committee of the European Communities, 2 rue Ravenstein, B-1000 Brussels, Belgium. Tel: 02 46 90 11 Fax: (02) 513 48 93 Email: info@esc.eu.int

Employment Conditions Abroad (ECA), Anchor House, 15–19 Britten Street, London SW3 3TY. Tel: (020) 7351 5000 Fax: (020) 7351 9396.

Federation of Recruitment and Employment Services Ltd, 36-38 Mortimer Street, London W1N 7RB Tel: (020) 7323 4300 Fax: (020) 7255 2878.

Inland Revenue Claims Branch, Merton Road, Bootle L69 9BL.

International Voluntary Service, Old Hall, East Bergholt, Colchester CO7 6TQ. Tel: (01206) 298215.

Independent Schools Information Service (ISIS), 35–37 Grosvenor Gardens, London SW1W 0BS. Tel: (020) 7798 1500.

Linguaphone, Carlton Plasa, 111 Upper Richmond Road;, London SW15 2TJ. Tel: (020) 8333 4900.

Lloyds TSB Group plc, Isle of Man Expatriate Centre, 7 Douglas St, Peel, Isle of Man. Tel: (01624) 638084 Fax: (01624) 843885.

Midland Bank plc, Expatriate Dept, New Street, St Helier, Jersey. Tel: (01534) 606920.

NatWest Expatriate Service, PO Box 12, 6 High Street, Chelmsford, Essex CM1 1BL. Tel: 0845 0011 2233.

Passport Agency, Clive House, 70 Petty France, London SW1H 9HD. Tel: 0870 521 0410.

Recruitment Section, Personnel Command, Foreign and Commonwealth Office, 1 Palace Street, London SWE 5HE. Tel: (020) 7270 1500 Fax: (020) 7839 2417 Email: pmd.fco@gtnet.gov.uk.

Survival Books, PO Box 146, Wetherby LS23 6XZ. Tel: (01937) 843523.

The Employment Service, Overseas Placing Unit, Level 5, Skills House, 3-7 Holy Green, Sheffield S1 4AQ. Tel: (0114) 259 6086.

The European Parliament (London Office), 2 Queen Anne's Gate, London SW1H 9AA. Tel: (020) 7227 4300.

United Nations: UNA Exchange, Temple of Peace, Cathays Park, Cardiff CF10 3AP. Tel: (029) 2022 3088.

Voluntary Service Overseas, 317 Putney Bridge Road, London SW15 2PN. Tel: (020) 8780 7200.

A FINAL WORD

The information in this book is accurate at the time of writing. However, details are subject to continual change and readers must confirm details for themselves before travelling abroad. In particular, be sure to check the work and residence permit regulations of each country with the respective embassy. When travelling abroad it is essential to take out suitable travel insurance, and enough money to support yourself on arrival and to pay for your return home if you do not find a job, or a pre-arranged job proves unsuitable.

Index